Achieve Cosmic Co

CW00470662

and

Live in Enlightenment

A New Commentary on the Bhagavad Gita
For Active People Engaged in Life

By Keith R Parker

Second Edition

Copyright

Cover: Brazilian graphics designer Samara Battisti weds NASA's image of deep space with unbounded Cosmic Consciousness.

GALATIANS 5:13

"You, my brothers and sisters, were called to be free. But do not use your freedom in sinful selfish acts; rather serve one another in selfless acts of love."

John Keats

"Wherein lies happiness? in that which becks
Our ready minds to fellowship divine,
A fellowship with essence; till we shine,
Full alchemiz'd, and free of space. Behold
The clear religion of heaven!"

Where would I be?

To Reny for love and unflinching support and my old friend William for critical turns.

Acknowledgement

All this blossoms from that. I use Maharishi Mahesh Yogi's translation and commentary on the *Bhagavad Gita* as one of my principal references. Maharishi's emphasis on turning the mind within to the field of least activity and my emphasis on the Yoga of action — the practice of Karma Yoga — led me to differ moderately in translation and substantially so in commentary. MMY emphasized pulling the arrow back on the bowstring to prepare for action. This practice of Karma Yoga is that action: the arrow flying forward. This cost-free, universal, independent, and direct means to achieving happiness in higher states of consciousness through the practice of Karma Yoga would please MMY no end.

Table of Contents

Introduction

Claim independence.

Karma Yoga is Krishna's declaration of independence from grinding away at spiritual growth in the slow lane. The practice liberates us from arcane philosophies, pilgrimages and retreats, crossing a Brahmin's palm with silver, the Vedas, proxy sacrifices, steep learning curves, living in a Himalayan cave, standing on our heads, spinning our wheels.

Rather, through the practice of Karma Yoga achieve liberation by merely taking on responsibilities of everyday life. Find virtue, fulfillment, balance of mind, skill in action, wisdom, and the groove of life. Quickly achieve Cosmic Consciousness through action alone. Experience inner contentment, peace of mind and happiness. See Oneness in all, feel familiar with all, know all. Spontaneously live your cosmic purpose to fully enjoy the nature of the cosmos. Emptiness filled. Be yourself.

All you need to know about realizing Cosmic Consciousness through the practice of Karma Yoga lies in Chapters 2, 3 and 4 of the *Bhagavad Gita*. The practice comes naturally. Time, place, experience, and religious commitments are irrelevant. Open to everyone, Karma Yoga is straightforward, effortless and without obstacles.

On the other hand, controlling the mind, disciplining the senses, resisting desires, restraining actions, and driving into *cul de sacs* of mood making — as taught in the canonical practice of Karma Yoga — have no place in Krishna's teaching and this revival of it.

Through the practice of Karma Yoga, Cosmic Consciousness quickly dawns. We identify with quiet inner contentment and naturally perform dynamic right actions that support spiritual and material evolution. Liberation from the sense of "I" and "mine" frees us from possessions and the need to possess. Peace of mind unchains us from the delusion of looking for happiness "out there" in the material world. In equanimity, the curtain falls on anxiety, sadness and distress. The light of happiness shines from within. We feel at home.

How to achieve Cosmic Consciousness through the practice of Karma Yoga? Do your duty. The practice naturally flows from living a responsible life. It is practiced by getting things done, not in a Himalayan cave free from obligations. It is practiced within social interactions, not in abstaining from them. It is practiced by taking the initiative and doing your best to serve those you honor and love, not by holding back, saving yourself for a better day.

You already practice Karma Yoga to some degree. You just do not know it. Knowing it lies in intellectually understanding the power of selfless actions (Ch 2) and directly experiencing the liberating quality of actions in service to others (Ch 3).

Understanding and experience work together, laying the foundation for knowledge. As understanding and experience enliven, support and strengthen each other, knowledge awakens from within. We feel the groove of service in daily activity. Right actions supporting spiritual and material evolution feel familiar and we spontaneously perform them.

Evolving understanding and experience bring knowledge to light (Ch 4). Through the practice, the fog of ignorance dissipates and we see the singular Oneness underlying all diversity in the universe. In seeing Oneness in all we become familiar with all. In familiarity with all, we know all. We feel at home. Our thoughts, feelings and actions tune into accomplishing cosmic purpose, which is to enjoy creation fully.

Gaining knowledge is merely a matter of integrating understanding and experience by getting on with life's responsibilities. By throwing yourself into life's demands, evolve. And therein lies the Supreme Secret to practicing Karma Yoga affirmed in Ch 2, 3 and 4 of the *Bhagavad Gita*: Do your duty. Duty alone takes us the distance to higher states of consciousness, Cosmic and beyond. Overviews for each chapter interleave salient points in plain English and familiarize the reader with the nitty-gritty detail of commentaries to follow.

Anyone living anywhere on God's Earth quickly and easily gains Cosmic Consciousness, simply by following Krishna's teaching in Ch 2, 3 and 4. Higher states of consciousness take more time, discipline and instruction. For those with clear experiences of Cosmic Consciousness, three appendices bring to light Krishna's teaching on achieving Brahman Consciousness (Ch 5), God Consciousness (Ch 6) and knowing God (Ch 7).

Because all three higher states of consciousness — Cosmic, Brahman and God — are readily achieved by those who endeavor to reach them, recognizing each state's experience helps acknowledge progress and maintain footholds gained. A final appendix summarizes — in a nutshell — the overarching experiences of higher states of consciousness as described by Krishna in the *Bhagavad Gita*.

Reading the *Bhagavad Gita* can be a bit daunting. Most start but never finish. True enough, some read the *Gita* from stem to stern. But by the time they finish, the boat of knowledge has sailed to deeper waters, where verses take on more profound meaning upon rereading. Hence to read the *Gita* is, in fact, to reread the *Gita*. Then too, the earnest seeker can get lost in integrating Krishna's vast expanse of wisdom into daily life. It can be too much of a good thing.

So instead of "reading" the *Gita*, most read "in" it. They favor meaningful verses. Integrating those verses into their daily lives, they start at their own level of consciousness and evolve at their own pace.

I take this approach by focusing on early chapters relevant to practicing Karma Yoga and achieving Cosmic Consciousness. Begin with "*Achieve Cosmic Consciousness in Five Key Verses.*" These verses contain all you need to learn the practice. Understand the commentary on these key verses through direct experience of the practice and you'll achieve quiet inner contentment in daily life.

Smooth the journey. "*Strengthen the Practice and Enrich the Experience*" integrates synergy between evolving understanding and experience. Practicing Karma Yoga and reading select verses of interest smooths rough spots of misunderstanding and hastens evolution.

The *Gita* verifies experience. Anyone who reads the *Gita* with a view toward their experiences will recognize within themselves experiences of higher states of consciousness the *Gita* describes. That is, anyone who wants to. My sincere hope: this commentary awakens awareness of those higher experiences within you.

Returning to favorite verses cultivates familiarity with experience and knowledge gained through understanding. Skip around among verses that interest you. Or far better, read all verses in Ch 2 (my commentary starts with verse 39), 3 and 4; it is a beautiful journey of growth in consciousness, consistently climbing higher and higher on the vertical plane of life. Ascend. Through understanding and experience, Cosmic Consciousness quickly dawns. Just follow your curiosity. Do your duty. Evolve at your own pace. You are your best guide.

I assume readers are somewhat familiar with the *Bhagavad Gita*'s storyline. If not, the narrative is told in conversation between Arjuna and Lord Krishna, Arjuna's charioteer, spiritual guide and Vishnu incarnate. Arjuna — the greatest archer of his time — is filled with moral dilemma and despair about having to kill kinsmen who stand opposing him on the field of battle, weapons at the ready. Divided between dictates of heart and mind, slumped on the seat of his chariot, Arjuna dithers on his dilemma and how to liberate himself from his predicament.

Krishna counsels Arjuna to take the path of action and do his duty. Through action alone, he will achieve quiet inner contentment in the state of Cosmic Consciousness, liberating himself from the consequences of action. Krishna admonishes, "Stand up and fight."

These early chapters of the *Gita* are not, in fact, about how Lord Krishna liberates Arjuna from the miseries of bondage to action. They are about you. They are about how understanding action (Ch 2) and experiencing Divine nature through sacrifice of desire (Ch 3) propel you toward familiarity with your inner nature and the knowledge of who you are deep within (Ch 4). Such is the beauty of the *Gita* that your course of reading is your course of evolution.

It is the cusp of battle. Blaring conch horns inspire unity and selfless actions. Death-tipped arrows will soon pierce the hearts and minds of men. Righteousness will prevail, or not. With no time to waist, Krishna lights the way and brings Arjuna up to unbounded dynamic action based on quiet inner contentment. Start with Achieve Cosmic Consciousness in Five Key Verses.

Achieve Cosmic Consciousness in Five Key Verses

"By action alone Perfection was gained," Lord Krishna.

These five verses provide the understanding and experience needed to practice Karma Yoga and evolve to Cosmic Consciousness. The practice naturally integrates quiet inner and outer dynamic aspects of our nature. Through daily activity, integration becomes established and a state of restful alertness coexists within all action.

Take the express train. Take the householder's path. Men and women of action naturally practice Karma Yoga in everyday life. Acting to serve others' desires, they innocently renounce their own. Desires renounced, they achieve inner contentment and perform actions free from attachments to objects of desire. Out of contentment, liberation from overpowering feelings, thoughts and actions.

All that is required to achieve Cosmic Consciousness through the practice of Karma Yoga is understanding the nature of desire and action, experiencing daily activity for the liberation that it is, and gaining knowledge. Naturally and easily done!

[Note: Chapter and verse are displayed as decimals. For example, verse 15 of chapter 3 is 3.15]

Links and abstracts to Five Key Verses:

Bound to actions

2.39. We get stuck in cycles of *impression-desire-action*. We *desire* an object's attractive qualities and take *action* to experience the happiness it promises — say, purchase a spiffy new car. In time, the experience of happiness wears thin and an *impression* of dissatisfaction sets in. We *desire* a new and different object to experience happiness, take *action* to acquire it and again in time, an *impression* of dissatisfaction. Bound to cycles of *impression-desire-action* to find happiness outside ourselves, we get nowhere fast in our incessant search for it.

Liberated from actions

2.45. When we selflessly serve others' desires, we innocently renounce our own. We break the cycle of *impression-desire-action* at the level of our selfish *desire* to find happiness outside ourselves. No selfish *desire*, no selfish *action*, no impression of *dissatisfaction*, no cycle of *impression-desire-action*. Liberated from bondage to action, our attention naturally turns away from the material world and its illusory promise of happiness. We find happiness within and arise out of the muck and muddle of bondage to action.

Act: do your duty

3.08. Do your duty! Meet your responsibilities. Serve the desires of those you honor and love. Naturally sacrifice desire. Cast away grinding cycles of *impression-desire-action*. Step forward onto the firm ground of inner contentment. Fulfilled, naturally perform right actions that support evolution in spiritual and material wellbeing for all, achieve balance of mind and gain skill in action. Do your duty: live the groove of service and evolve to the highest levels of spiritual and material wellbeing.

Sacrifice desire: get creative

3.15. Sacrifice *with*, not *to*. All selfless acts that sacrifice desire are born in creation arising from the unmanifest field of all possibilities, supporting only good, increase and evolution. Consequently, this primal force of creation infuses sacrifice of desire, enlivening sacrificial acts, enhancing separation of Self from desire and action, furthering evolution in spiritual and material wellbeing, and rendering support of Nature.

Feel familiar with all: know all

4.33. Seeing transcendent Oneness in all, we become familiar with all, we know all. The familiar feeling of quiet contentment within while engaged in dynamic outer activity verifies the practice of Karma Yoga. Through continued verification, liberation of higher Self from action evolves into higher experiences of separation from this and that. Disconnected experiences of separation unite into a pervasive vision of separation from all else. All else unites into an omnipresent Oneness that feels right and familiar. We achieve an awareness of something good and fundamental pervading all. In this way, we know all.

Strengthen the Practice and Enrich the Experience

"God is in the details," Ludwig Mies van der Rohe.

Take a deeper dive. The following concepts link to verses that synergize understanding and experience, smooth the journey, and hasten evolution to Cosmic Consciousness.

[Note: Chapter and verse are displayed as decimals. For example, verse 15 of chapter 3 is 3.15.]

ACTION — Fulfill desires:

Desire seeds action. In waking-state consciousness, we act on individual needs for survival and gain. When we serve others' desires and achieve steady intellect — when we practice Karma Yoga — liberation from selfish desires and emotional attachments opens the door to acting on Nature's desires. In Cosmic Consciousness, Nature's desires seed actions for spiritual and material evolution.

2.39: Suffer bondage to action.

2.45: Achieve liberation from action.

2.47: Naturally perform right actions.

3.15: Partner with the act of creation.

3.20: Gain perfection in action.

4.23, 4.36 – 4.38: Dissolve consequence of action.

ANGER — Anger destroys intellect:

Sitting on a high stool, faced into the dark corner of ignorance, dunce cap and all. Contrary to popular belief, anger does not motivate. Rather, anger incapacitates.

2.62 – 2.63: Understanding: Desire gives rise to anger.

3.37: Experience: It's a car wreck.

4.10: Knowledge: Dissolve anger in the austerity of knowledge.

APPEARANCES — It's hard to tell:

What's inside counts.

2.46 – 2.53: Experience underlying properties of union (Yoga).

2.54: Live the persona of Cosmic Consciousness.

2.55 – 2.56: Rise above selfish desire and emotional attachments.

2.57 – 2.71: Achieve inner nature of Cosmic Consciousness.

AUSTERITY — Liberation from desires:

In higher Self we live austere to worldly pleasures of lower self.

4.10: Purify by the austerity of knowledge.

4.11: Travel the path of austerity to austerity.

4.13 – 4.14: Reach the highest austerity of all: non-doing in higher states of consciousness.

BONDAGE TO ACTION — Senses connect us to objects of desire:

2.39: Stuck in cycles of unfulfilling action.

2.45: Liberation from bondage.

3.25: Act without bondage.

3.31: Attraction and aversion reinforce bondage.

CONTROL — Put inner contentment in control:

We control from within. In union, higher Self infuses its Absolute contented nature into lower self. In this way, contented higher Self naturally controls intellect, mind and senses of lower self. Contrary to popular belief, control means neither resisting desire nor restraining actions nor remaining indifferent to outcomes. Instead, let go. Serve others' desires, innocently renounce your own and experience Absolute control come naturally.

2.61: Control the wavering mind by inner contentment.

2.64 - 2.66: Render happiness through spontaneous Self-control.

3.06 - 3.07: Free yourself from delusion of control and hypocrisy of wrong action.

3.33: What can restraint accomplish?

COSMIC CONSCIOUSNESS — Deep within desires no longer occur:

Where waking-state consciousness is awareness caught up in experience, Cosmic Consciousness is awareness separate from experience. Quiet and content deep within, we experience desires, thoughts and emotions on the surface of the mind. We witness the organs of action act and life unfold to higher Truths of our inner nature.

2.57: Calm and content deep within, rule your turbulent nature.

2.69: Witness waking, sleeping and dreaming.

2.64 – 2.66: Realize peace of mind and happiness from within.

2.71: Experience life free from the sense of "I" and "mine."

2.72: Live attributes of CC summarized in verses 2.57 - 2.71.

COSMIC PURPOSE — Universal happiness in universal good:

"And God saw everything He had made and behold, it was good," — *Genesis*. Cosmic purpose is to fully enjoy the nature of the cosmos. All creation is good and supports evolution to fully realize the universal nature of happiness within it.

4.18: Cosmic purpose informs wisdom.

4.20: Wisdom informs action.

4.21: Act without sin.

DHARMA — Go with the flow, practice Karma Yoga:

Dharma is your path of action to final liberation.

2.40: Your dharma is to practice Karma Yoga.

3.16: Follow the wheel set revolving.

3.35: Be yourself, actualize dharma.

4.08: The sinful sow the seeds of their destruction.

DUTY — Krishna's teaching:

In the master stroke of performing one's duty, sacrifice desire, break bondage to action and know thy Self.

3.08: Practice Karma Yoga.

3.31: What exactly is Krishna's teaching?

3.35: Be yourself.

4.15: Duty has an excellent track record. "Just Do It" — *Nike*.

INTELLECT & EGO — Gain power of discernment:

2.39: Discern reality and who you really are.

2.50: I am unbounded inner contentment of Self.

2.55: Steady intellect.

2.57: Established Intellect.

KNOWLEDGE — See Oneness in all, know all:

According to *Merriam-Webster* online dictionary: "knowledge is the fact or condition of knowing something with *familiarity* (author's emphasis) gained through experience or association." See Oneness in all, become familiar with all, know all.

4.31: Taste the sweet nectar of familiarity with all.

4.33: Practice the Yoga more equal than others.

4.36: The past, it just makes sense.

4.37: Live in the present: consequence begone.

4.38: Purify imperfections with knowledge alone.

4.39: Devote yourself to duty, devote yourself to pursuit of knowledge.

4.41: Cut away doubt.

4.42: Swing the sword of knowledge.

ONENESS — Common ground in all creation:

We see Oneness in everything.

4.18: Unifying Oneness pervades all.

4.19: Eliminate desire and incentive.

4.21: Incur no sin.

4.24: Karma Yoga is the great opportunity: offering, oblation and fire wrapped up in a single act of service.

4.31: Taste the yummy nectar of familiarity.

SACRIFICE (of desire) — The high road to liberation:

Sacrifice of desire furthers evolution. When we practice Karma Yoga by sacrificing our desires to serve others' desires, we instantly sacrifice fears, sorrows, distress, emotional pain, suffering, turbulent senses, wavering mind, jittery intellect, doubts, concerns for success and failure, prejudice, selfish attitudes, sinful thoughts … all that retard evolution through wrong actions, attachments, and possessions and the need to possess. All this troublesome petty individuality flies out the open window and we inhale the pure air of the universal Self. Smiles all around.

3.09: Enjoy the universe's free lunch.

3.10: You can run but you can't hide: it's in your DNA.

3.11: On Team Evolution play the position of gratitude.

3.12: Gratitude wins in a knockout punch.

3.14: Sacrifice desire, trump Vedic petition.

3.15: Sacrifice desire *with* Brahma, not *to* Brahma.

4.24: In Karma Yoga, see Oneness, gain familiarity and realize knowledge of all.

SECRET — The Supreme Secret of Ancient Yoga:

Society loses the practice of Karma Yoga to the passage of time.

4.01 – 4.03: Where to hide the Supreme Secret?

4.04 – 4.07: He Is what He Is and He does His Thing!

4.08 – 4.09: The consequences of wrong actions dim in the light of knowledge.

SELF — Lower self is action; Higher Self is:

Simultaneously live bounded lower self in union with unbounded higher Self.

2.39 (Yoga): Lose the forest for the trees.

2.45 (Union): Infuse bounded lower self with unbounded higher Self.

2.61, 2.64: Discipline relative ever changing within Absolute never changing.

SUPPORT OF NATURE — In league with Nature:

You get what you need when you need it to further spiritual and material evolution. Like it or not.

2.51: Act on Nature's desires.

3.11: Trust in Nature.

3.12: Let it be: Nature knows best.

3.15: Tap into the power of creation.

4.18: Take on cosmic responsibility, receive cosmic support.

VIRTUE — Enliven moral Being:

Instinctive moral and ethical guidance of mind and character fosters virtuous behavior, balance of mind and spiritual evolution.

2.45 (Cardinal Virtues): See moral and ethical values blossom in the light of inner contentment.

3.08: Experience duty sow the seeds of virtuous action.

3.25: *Sans* virtue, teeter on the edge of dystopia.

WISDOM — Act on Nature's desire:

Wisdom is action taken to fulfill Nature's desire to further spiritual and material evolution. Wisdom is neither a matter of sound judgment nor a matter of deliberately discerning right from wrong nor a matter of experience nor a matter of intellectual understanding nor the product of contemplation and compassion. Instead, wisdom is the instinctive ability to perform Nature's desires.

2.51 - 2.52: Act on Nature's desire to follow your path of evolution.

3.25: Fulfill the welfare of the world.

3.39: Beware the insatiable flame of desire.

4.18 - 4.19: With the fire of knowledge, burn the evil side of desire to a crisp.

Chapter 2 — Understand Renunciation of Desire

Overview of Ch 2:

In Cosmic Consciousness, awareness maintains itself during waking, dreaming and sleeping states of consciousness. We witness desires, thoughts and actions go of their own accord. We live in the groove of life. We achieve Cosmic Consciousness by practicing Karma Yoga: serving others' desires. In serving others' desires, we innocently renounce our own desires and the selfish actions they seed. In selfless actions, we identify with inner contentment and experience fulfillment, perform spontaneous right actions and achieve balance of mind. Strong emotions lose their grip. Quiet and content deep within, we witness desires on the surface of the mind and the organs of action act. We gain indifference to the sense of "I" and "mine," freeing us from the delusion of looking for happiness "out there" in the material world. Peace of mind ends anxiety and overpowering emotions of sadness and distress. Happiness from within dominates. We feel at home, like slipping a foot into a comfortable old shoe.

This chapter's commentaries start with verse 39, the point where Krishna shifts gears from philosophy to the practice of Karma Yoga.

Bondage to action: 39 We bind to our never-ending and fruitless actions to find lasting happiness in the material world. Attached to attractive qualities found in objects of the senses we become bound to our actions. In its search for happiness, ever-active lower self overshadows the contented nature of higher Self. Bondage to actions puts the brakes on living our full potential in Cosmic Consciousness. 40 The practice of Karma Yoga breaks bondage to action. Effortless and obstacle free, the practice points us along our dharmic path to higher spiritual and material wellbeing. 41 Resolute and one-pointed in the practice, we see possibilities, an order to our lives and a rewarding course of action forward.

Selfish action: 42 On the other hand, the irresolute who fail to practice Karma Yoga confuse spiritual evolution with material gain. They praise the literal language of Vedic laws governing actions, convinced there is no deeper meaning than material gain. 43 Seeing selfish desire and action as the means to liberation, they believe happiness lies in wealth and power. To them, actions reward rebirth into higher seats of material gain. They lose sight of the vertical plane of life and final liberation. 44 The irresolute skip from one enjoyment and exercise of power to the next, deepening bondage to action. Under the grip of selfish desire and action, they navigate life as a rudderless ship charges through rock-strewn, foggy seas.

Selfless action: 45 The practice of Karma Yoga liberates us from bondage to action and points the way to higher spiritual and material wellbeing. When we selflessly serve others' desires, we instantly break with selfish desire to find happiness in objects of the senses. Selfish desire renounced and liberated from bondage to action, the mind naturally turns inward towards the unbounded source of happiness that lies within. We identify with our Real and True nature: unbounded inner contentment of higher Self. Bounded lower self unites within unbounded higher Self. Our selfless actions feel spontaneous and right, easy and familiar. Cardinal virtues blossom. We experience liberation even in the simplest selfless acts of service. 46 Our cup runneth over in fulfillment born of Self's inner contentment. Prescribed Vedic laws governing actions have no more use than a well in a place flooded by water on all sides. 47 Rather, we spontaneously perform right actions that support evolution in spiritual and material wellbeing, obviating sinful wrong actions. In time, steady inner contentment of higher Self underlies all actions. 48 Out of equilibrium of contented Self, we achieve balance of mind in success and failure, progress and reversal, ups and downs, and all dualities of life. We feel at home.

Liberated from action: 49 In union with higher Self, the intellect naturally discerns reality and truth, showing the way toward achievement. On the other hand, emotional attachments hold sway over those motivated by selfish desire. They ride a rollercoaster of ups-and-downs and twist-and-turns. Going round and round, they produce little of lasting value and stumble along their path of evolution, at best. 50 But devoted to the practice of Karma Yoga, we cast away actions that retard evolution. Spontaneously renouncing desire and innocently performing selfless actions that foster evolution, we achieve skill in action and readily achieve outcomes.

Wisdom: 51 For the wise happiness comes from within, eliminating the need for ephemeral happiness born of fruits of action. Having innocently renounced desire for the fruits of actions, where do desires come from? Ans: Nature. We wisely act on Nature's desire to further spiritual and material evolution. Wisdom indeed: spontaneous action in accord with Nature receives Nature's support. We live in a state free from suffering. 52&53 Bypassing Vedic doctrine for guidance on action, we spontaneously live in the present of selfless actions seeded by Nature's purpose to further spiritual and material evolution. Acting on Nature's desires, we become established in Yoga, union of lower self within higher Self.

54 How does union of lower self within higher Self and performing actions in accord with Nature reveal itself? What are the outward signs of inner contentment? How does someone with balanced mind and skilled in action speak, sit and move? That is, how would we know one if we saw one?

Steady intellect: 55&56 During the practice of Karma Yoga we cast off desires that have gone deep within the mind. We achieve inner contentment. Intellect steadies. Content within, emotional attachments, fear and anger depart. Fulfilled within, spontaneous right actions fulfill outcomes.

Established intellect: 57 In time, steady intellect achieved in Karma Yoga establishes itself in the unbounded nature of higher Self. Awareness remains uninvolved with cognitive and physical activity. We rise above overindulgence in joy and sadness upon experiencing pleasant and unpleasant outcomes. We live in evenness of rock-solid higher Self. 58&59 In all actions, we are an island unto the Self. Self-sufficient, even the taste for attractive qualities found in objects of the senses drop away. Senses, mind and intellect operate in accord with Nature. Cooler heads prevail.

Control: 60 Resisting the turbulent senses sustains desire and deepens bondage to action. For those earnestly endeavoring to resist them, the turbulent senses carry away the mind. Jittery lower self overshadows contented higher Self. 61 On the other hand, fulfilling inner contentment of higher Self outcompetes fleeting happiness promised in attractive qualities found in objects of the senses. In this way, calming inner contentment of higher Self effortlessly "controls" senses, mind and intellect of lower self, innocently maintaining right action, freedom from attachments, balance of mind, and skill in action. Calmness and an even attitude prevail.

Anger: 62 On the other hand, possessiveness, cravings, frustration, and anger arise from pondering on objects of the senses and the unattainable lasting happiness they promise. 63 To justify our anger, we create a false narrative. Imagination outcompetes reality and intellect dysfunctions in its ability to choose wisely. As a result, we disengage from the natural rhythms of life and flounder on the hard rocks of reality.

Happiness: 64 Having established intellect in the Self, we disengaged from attachment, fear, desire, and anger. We move among the objects of the senses under the control of contented higher Self. We naturally disengage from attractions and aversions that overshadow Self. We find inner peace. 65 Inner peace protects the mind from attachments, aversions, possessions, and the need to possess. Frustrations, anger and sorrows depart. We find peace of mind within. 66 Out of peace of mind, Self-control, steady thought, established intellect, and happiness.

Withdraw senses from their objects: 67 Having failed to achieve lasting happiness, wandering senses carry away the mind as wind carries away a ship on water. We spin our wheels. 68 But intellect established in the rock-solid higher Self achieved through the practice of Karma Yoga, the wandering senses withdraw from their objects. The pull of attractions and aversions attenuates. The overshadowing nature of petty lower self gives way to contented higher Self.

Live Cosmic Consciousness: 69 We experience the continuity of contented higher Self separate from action, experiencing awareness of waking, sleeping, dreaming, and separation from feelings, thoughts and action. 70 Fulfilled in inner contentment of Self, desires enter the mind as waters enter the full and undisturbed sea. Desires appear on the surface of the mind, seeding the organs of action to act of their own accord to achieve higher levels of spiritual and material wellbeing. In separation from the field of action, we attain peace of mind and happiness. 71 We abandon attachments and live independent of the sense of 'I' and 'mine.' Reliance on possessions to achieve lasting happiness loses sway. Longing for fruits of actions depart. 72 Freed from the delusion of finding happiness "out there" in objects of the senses, universal higher Self holds sway over petty individual lower self, attachments and bondage to action. This is Cosmic Consciousness: Self separate from action. Lower self at peace within Self-sufficient higher Self. Freedom reigns in happiness experienced.

Commentary on Ch 2 verses 39 - 72:

Bondage to action:

2.39. Lord Krishna: *Having heard the philosophical understanding of Samkhya, now hear my teaching applied to Yoga. Your intellect established through the practice of it, you will cast away the bondage of karma* [the bondage to action].

Here, Krishna shifts gears from theoretical to practical, from philosophy to action. Through Samkhya's philosophy on consciousness and cognition (previous verses), Krishna has instructed Arjuna not to fear death. Only by fearlessly performing his duty will Arjuna liberate himself from incurring sin and the miserably dithering and indecisive state he finds himself in.

This foundational verse identifies the goal of liberation and lays out the obstacles to achieving it.

Karma and Yoga: Karma means action. First and foremost, karma means taking action to liberate oneself from the '*bondage of karma,*' from the bondage to action.

Yoga means union of lower self within higher Self. The lower self ever-changes, perishable; the higher Self never-changes, imperishable, eternal. The lower self is bounded individuality of senses, mind, intellect, and ego; the higher Self is Absolute unbounded universal contentment. The lower self lives in time and space; the higher Self exists outside the passage of time and just is. The lower self achieves outcomes and bears their consequences; the higher Self exists free from outcomes and consequences. We know the lower self in our everyday experiences by names like Arden, Blair and Charlie; we know the higher Self by achieving inner contentment. For the strong mind, lower self unites within higher Self and takes on its Absolute and unbounded qualities.

For the weak mind, lower self binds to endless, fruitless actions to find happiness in objects of desire. Bound to the rollercoaster ups-and-downs and twists-and-turns to find happiness "out there" in the material world, the excitable lower self overshadows the steady nature of higher Self. We lose the forest for the trees. Individuality overrides universality. Life suffers. Conflicts and frustrations arise. Infrequently, life is smooth and rewarding, as we instinctively know it should be. We more often scratch across the grooves of life than find ourselves merrily tapping a foot in tune with it.

Intellect to the rescue: '*Your intellect established through the practice of*' Karma Yoga, achieve union of lower self within higher Self, achieve Yoga. *Definitions*: intellect discerns between true and false; ego — the subtlest quality of intellect — discerns who we truly are. Through the practice of Karma Yoga, we strengthen ego and identify with the ultimate Truth: I am unbounded Self. Unbounded includes all that is bound. The bounded lower self unites within higher Self and takes on its Absolute contented nature.

In union of lower self within higher Self, conflicts and frustrations dissipate. We no longer rely on actions to achieve happiness through material gain. We do not have to. Content deep within, we remain at peace on the level of Absolute Self. Out of inner peace, happiness.

We no longer rely on action to achieve happiness in objects of desire. No action, no binding influence of it. Liberated. We '*cast away the bondage of karma*,' the bondage to action.

Bondage of Karma: We become bound to our actions when desires connect the senses with attractive qualities found in objects of sensory experience. The sight of a spiffy new Porsche, touch of silk, sound of enchanting music, alluring scent of perfume, and feel of new running shoes capture attention and pull mind, intellect and ego out into the ever-changing, relative field of life.

In a sense, desire suckers the weak mind into thinking we have arrived. The happiness we seek in some sensory experience is the real deal. We are there: '*I have found the lasting happiness I have always sought.*' Or so we think. Or rather, so we imagine.

Through the office of desire, imagination takes over. Seeing an ad for vacationing in Bora Bora, we imagine running through the surf, cool water splashing our sun-warmed skin, the scent of hibiscus, a Bahama Mama sucked through a long straw poked into a coconut.

The mind's imagined sensory experiences and a busy feeling of progress gained by strategizing on attaining them capture our attention and overshadow our ability to discern Reality and Truth. That is, imagination and feelings of progress overshadow the ego's identity with unbounded Absolute Self. The ego loses sight of who we really are, unbounded inner contentment, Absolute Self.

All-powerful desire hijacks refined qualities of mind, intellect and ego, and drags them "out there" to where we think we'll find happiness in the everchanging relative field of life. This, even though we full-well know that contentment and lasting happiness lie within. We get all involved in the lower self's desires, thoughts, strategies, and actions to attain the object of desire. The deep-rooted and steady nature of ego identified with Absolute Self gets caught up in the everchanging.

We take *action* to acquire the desired object and experience the happiness it promises. But in time, the object loses allure. Failure to find lasting happiness — say, in Bora Bora — registers an *impression* of dissatisfaction deep within the mind. A *desire* arises to take *action* anew and find happiness in some different object of the senses, say, a new pair of running shoes. Desire seeds action anew. We buy the running shoes, go for a run and experience measures of happiness. But again, in time, happiness wears thin and we experience an impression of dissatisfaction.

This binding influence of action fixes us to a cycle of *impression-desire-action*. Bound to our actions, our attention flows ever outward away from inner contentment and lasting happiness, the very goals sought in taking action in the first place. This is bondage to action. Since Karma means action, this is '*bondage of karma.*'

2.40. *In practicing Karma Yoga no effort is forfeited and no obstacle to completion exists. A little of this dharma protects one from great peril.*

"I've been in my mind; it's such a fine line; that keeps me searching for a heart of gold," Neal Young. Dharma is the omnipresent magnetic field of evolution flowing through us, guiding us to higher spiritual and material wellbeing. In practicing Karma Yoga, we immerse ourselves into the flowing field of dharma and quickly evolve to those higher levels. Our dharma is to practice Karma Yoga.

'*No effort is forfeited*' because to break the bondage to action (previous verse) merely requires trading selfish desires for selfless ones (2.45). Achieving liberation far exceeds any effort expended in switching between the two. In confidence, we step effortlessly along our path.

'*No obstacle to completion exists*' because the practice of Karma Yoga is in our DNA and comes naturally to us (3.10). We were born to practice Karma Yoga, to serve those we honor and love. In performing it, we break '*bondage of karma*' (previous verse) and instantly achieve measures of liberation. So how can an '*obstacle*' obstruct our progress when we achieve our goal in each step taken?

Step-by-step liberation delivers from the '*great peril*' of instinctively knowing liberation from action exists but not understanding how to attain it. Even a little of this practice of Karma Yoga liberates us from the great peril of bondage to action. Quickly the scales fall from our eyes. We see possibilities and an order to things that protect us '*from great peril*' of forever being bound to our actions.

2.41. *In practicing Karma Yoga, the resolute intellect is focused, Arjuna, but the intellects of the irresolute have many branches and are infinitely various.*

In practicing Karma Yoga, we break bondage to action. Higher Self outshines excited and jittery lower self. Under the influence of Absolute Self, intellect steadies, discerns what is Real and True, and resolutely points us along our dharmic path to higher spiritual and material wellbeing (previous verse).

For non-practitioners, attractive qualities found in objects of sensory experience overshadow intellect. Non-practitioners, who are bound to actions to find happiness in objects of desire, forgo the intellect's steady powers of discernment gained in practicing Karma Yoga. Unresolved in intellect, attractive qualities in objects of the senses pull mind and intellect from one unfulfilling desire and action to the next (the cycle of impression-desire-action, 2.39). *'But the intellects of the irresolute'* non-practitioners, forever seeking happiness outside themselves, travel *'infinitely various'* paths to nowhere.

Selfish action:

2.42. *Absorbed in the letter of the Veda the indiscriminating proclaim there is no deeper meaning and speak flowery words.*

In their myopic vision, *'the indiscriminating'* exercise poor judgment (non-practitioners, previous verse). *'Absorbed in the letter of the Veda'* they see only what they can, the Vedas literal language but not its spirit. Through Vedic rites, they see only selfish ends and seek greater material wellbeing to achieve happiness and liberation from bondage. *Sans* the spirit of the Vedas, their endless quest for more focuses vision on text only. Biased to see enduring happiness within attractive qualities found in objects of the senses, they *'declare there is no deeper meaning'* to the Vedas than the letter of it.

The problem is, without complementary growth in spiritual wellbeing, acquiring material wealth holds those *'absorbed in the letter'* to the horizontal plane. Irresolute in intellect (previous verse) and self-deluded about the Vedas, *'the indiscriminating'* seek ever greater material wealth to gain happiness. In their never-ending quest for satisfaction through material possessions, they fix themselves to the cycle of impression-desire-action (2.39) and wander about in swamp-sucking disappointment, mistakenly seeing selfish petitionary action as the key to liberation.

Ignorance really is bliss. Bondage is its own safe space. Attractive qualities found in objects of the senses offer fleeting degrees of happiness and liberation. Seeing the Vedas as only a means to liberation through the attainment of material wealth and power, '*the indiscriminating*' demonstrate the shallowness of their understanding. They speak '*flowery words*' to reassure themselves and convince others to join their folly. Misery loves company.

2.43. *Full of selfish desires and intent on heavenly rewards, they offer rebirth as the reward for action and are addicted to Vedic rites for attaining enjoyment and power.*

'*Absorbed in the letter of the Veda*' (previous verse) leaves one '*full of selfish desires*' for more, which refuel dissatisfaction born of action to seek happiness in the material world (2.39). Fixed on the horizontal plane through selfish desires, '*the indiscriminating*' (previous verse) see action as the agency to '*rebirth*' and increase in '*heavenly rewards.*' They see the Vedas only to increase '*enjoyment and power*' — not to rise through all levels of evolution and live in contented Absolute Self.

Focused on '*the letter of the Veda*' and seduced by their own '*flowery words*' (previous verse), the undiscerning favor petitionary Vedic actions. They lose sight of the vertical plane and final liberation from bondage. Instead, they choose seductive pleasures bearing bondage.

2.44. *Steady intellect does not arise in those obsessed with enjoyment and power and firmly fascinated by their own flowery words.*

We gain *'steady intellect'* by the ego identified with Absolute Self (following verse). Therefore, *'steady intellect does not arise'* in the minds of those possessed by selfish desires who identify with the vicissitudes of *'enjoyment and power'* (previous verse). Attention held by attractive qualities found in objects of the senses, the irresolute live on the horizontal plane in the letter of the Vedas (2.42). Senses, mind, intellect, and ego skip from one *'enjoyment'* and exercise of *'power'* to the next, stemming steady cognitive powers born of inner contentment.

'Fascinated by their own flowery words' speaks volumes to the delusion of seeking lasting happiness outside ourselves in the relative field of life. Deep in our heart-of-hearts, we know eternal happiness lies within and that *'enjoyment and power'* turn attention in the opposite direction to the steady nature of contented Self. And yet, having neither experienced liberation from action nor gained an understanding of how to engender it, those who seek *'steady intellect'* through selfish petitionary Vedic action are rudderless and lost at sea under a foggy mist of ignorance.

The following verse lifts the veil of ignorance.

Selfless action:

2.45. *The three Gunas of Nature sustain the Vedas, Arjuna. Be without the three Gunas, liberated from life's dualities, fixed in purity, free of possessiveness, possessed of the Self.*

Cut to the chase: *'Be without the three Gunas.'*

Three Gunas: The Three Gunas of Nature underly all action — (1) Rajas | spur, (2) Sattva | development and direction, and (3) Tamas | check or retard. The Gunas uphold all creation, in all things and all ways. The Gunas create, develop and dissolve one stage of reality flowing into the next. Since all actions stem from the Gunas of Nature, '*The Veda's concern* [with specific actions to achieve liberation] *is with the three Gunas.*'

Be without the three Gunas: "All for freedom. Freedom for all." — *Harley-Davidson.* Arjuna is the all-time poster boy for getting all wrapped around the axle. To snap Arjuna out of his obsession with affecting right and wrong action, Krishna instructs him to be without action: '*Be without the three Gunas.*' On the level of higher Self, be without action and its consequences (2.39).

Krishna's teaching is a masterstroke of simplicity and effectiveness: to achieve the best course of action, be without action. Live on the level of higher Self and go with the flow of Nature to further evolution (2.51). Do not look for solutions to issues of righteous right and sinful wrong action on the level of action itself. Renounce action, else dissolve into a puddle of cowardliness, dithering and inaction.

Renunciation of action: We cannot do two things at once. The moment we act to fulfill others' desires, we break the cycle of impression-desire-action at the level of our desire to find happiness in the material world (2.39). We transcend desire, action and the relative field of life. No selfish desire, no selfish action ('*Be without the three Gunas*'), no impression of dissatisfaction to spur desire and action anew. Renouncing our desires and the actions they seed by selflessly serving others' desires is the practice of Karma Yoga.

Desireless and liberated from action and bondage to it, the outward flow of attention to find happiness "out there" in the material world stops dead in its tracks. The omnipresent flow of dharma turns awareness within toward more refined levels of contentment and happiness. At the finest level of awareness, the ego identifies with our ultimate Reality and Truth. *Sans* distractions of the material world, we realize our true nature. We are unbounded inner contentment of Absolute Self.

Union (Yoga): We achieve union of bounded outer activity (lower self) within the unbounded nature of contentment (higher Self). Inner contentment just is, non-dimensional, unchanging, Absolute, unbounded. By definition, the unbounded includes all that is bound. Bounded lower self unites within unbounded higher Self. Feeling, thinking and acting (self) coexists within all-pervading universal contentment (Self). Unboundedness of higher Self infuses individual mind, intellect and ego.

In union, desires fail to drag refined qualities of mind, intellect and ego out into the ever-changing field of reality. Thus, we experience desires on the surface of the mind; deep within, desires no longer occur. This is the experience of union (or Yoga): simultaneously maintaining never-changing inner contentment of higher Self while engaged in dynamic outer activity of lower self.

Cardinal virtues: In union, lower self takes on qualities of higher Self and we feel comfortable, secure and familiar with all. The glow of inner contentment infuses actions. Moral and ethical values blossom.

• We are *'liberated from life's dualities'* of disunion between lower self and higher Self. Outer and inner live in harmonious union of inner contentment. Tugs of heart (feelings) and mind (logic) cease to whipsaw us into conflicting feelings, thoughts and actions that wear us down. Life's dualities of success and failure, progress and reversal, ups and downs, easy and hard … release their grip in the glow of fulfilling inner contentment. Freed from fear engendered by life's dualities, virtues of courage and fortitude flourish.

• *'Liberated from life's dualities'* [ups and downs, progress and reversal, success and failure, right and wrong, happiness and sadness, hot and cold, in the groove and out of tune] we operate from refined levels of inner awareness *'fixed in purity'* of selfless intention to serve others. Harmful wrong actions retarding evolution fall away. In the contented nature of Self, *'purity'* of right actions supporting evolution prevails. Virtues of prudence and discernment to take a course of action supporting evolution come naturally.

• *'Fixed in purity'* and content deep within, we feel fulfilled. In need of nothing, self-worth exists *'free of possessiveness.'* Attachments begone. We cast away the burden of tightly holding onto what we have and the need to possess what others have. We break free from emotional attachments to outcomes, exercise positive aspects of our personality and enjoy life in actions we take. *'Free of possessiveness'* and liberated from selfish attitudes of avarice and envy, virtues of just and right actions naturally come to the fore.

• Inner contentment of higher Self pervades and illuminates all action. *'Free of possessiveness'* the glow of calm inner contentment governs feelings, thoughts and actions. Balanced in the equanimity of Self we act dynamically and skillfully, readily achieving outcomes. *'Possessed of the Self,'* rather than possessed by objects of desire, the virtue of Self-control comes from within, tempering appetition and moderating strong desires of lust, longing, attachment, and need.

Practice: It is not called a "practice" for nothing. Achieve Cosmic Consciousness through the practice of Karma Yoga. Each time we serve others' desires, we experience steady intellect and union of self within Self. Depth and duration of experience depend on strength of mind. Continued practice of Karma Yoga — renouncing desire by serving others' desires — strengthens the mind and enlivens experiences of higher Self and the harmonious union of lower self within it. In time, we fully identify with higher Self and become established in union, established in Yoga.

Test drive: Take the practice of Karma Yoga for a test drive. Perform some simple act of service: set the table for your mom, hold the door open for a burdened colleague, make a cup of tea for a friend. In the snap of a finger, liberation from bondage to action, feelings of inner wellbeing and smiles all around.

2.46. *All the Vedas are of no more value than is a small well flooded by water on every side for the Brahmana who knows.*

The '*Brahmana who knows*' lives in quiet inner awareness of Absolute Self, unmoved by actions and their consequences, knowing the Self is separate from all activity.

Once arrived, what use is a roadmap? Beyond action and in the fulfilling nature of contented Self, the Brahmana's "cup runneth over" in liberation from bondage to action. So, what use are step-by-step Vedic instructions for achieving liberation? Being without the three Gunas (previous verse), *'All the Vedas are of no more value than is a small well flooded by water on every side.'*

Rather than pursue prescribed Vedic actions, right actions come naturally (following verse).

2.47. You have control over action, not its fruits. Therefore, neither live for the fruits of action nor attach yourself to inaction.

'*You have control over action.*' You are in the driver's seat. Choose to act selflessly and foster evolution in spiritual and material wellbeing, right action. Or choose to act selfishly and hamper evolution, wrong action. Perform right actions and readily accomplish outcomes benefiting all. Perform wrong actions and leave outcomes to other fates.

Right and wrong actions: Selfless right actions further evolution. Practicing Karma Yoga is right action (2.45). Selflessly serving others' desires, we break bondage to action and realize inner contentment of higher Self. Spontaneously '*liberated from life's dualities,*' '*fixed in purity,*' '*freed from possessiveness,*' '*possessed of the Self*' (Cardinal virtues, 2.45), we naturally act in accord with Nature to further evolution.

In performing right actions, the uplifting feeling of liberation fuels us forward through thick and thin. Content deep within, unmindful of outcomes, while simultaneously motivated to achieve them, we pour single-minded attention into accomplishing tasks that need doing. Playing heads-up ball, we remain instinctively aware of what's important and unmindful of what's not. Fulfilled (previous verse), we make decisions without regard to loss and gain. Feeling harmony between quiet inner awareness and outer activity, the path of action to higher levels of wellbeing rolls out in front of us.

On the other hand, selfish wrong actions impede growth in spiritual and material wellbeing. By engaging in wrong actions, we become a negative force. Wrong actions harm others; hinder achieving outcomes; produce stress, strain and damaging influences on others and our environment; diminish the greater good of past right actions. Wrong actions result from selfish attitudes of avarice, anger, fear, revenge, and elitism. Selfishness points attention outwards and opposes the inward pull of dharma toward greater happiness (2.40). Consequently, selfish attitudes and wrong actions reinforce bondage to action and distance us from life-supporting right actions and evolution.

The good news: selfless right actions obviate selfish, wrong actions. Mutually exclusive right and wrong actions cannot co-occur. Inner contentment from selfless actions leaves no room for negative emotions, bad attitudes and selfish wrong actions. Favor right actions, that is, practice Karma Yoga.

Fruits of action: Putting attention on '*fruits of action*,' we siphon energy away from actions to achieve them. We miss opportunities and become less attentive and effective than we could otherwise be. We focus on the horizontal plane of material rewards and lose sight of the vertical and the purpose of action, which is liberation from bondage to it (2.45).

'*Nor attach yourself to inaction.*' Action is the name of the game. It is called Karma Yoga, the yoga of action. Attached to inaction, we become lethargic and fall asleep at the wheel. We numb ourselves to the joys of action and accomplishment. As contradictory as it sounds, liberation from bondage to action requires action. No selfless right action to break action's binding influence, no evolution, no peace of mind, no happiness (2.66). Favor right actions, that is, practice Karma Yoga.

Practice makes perfect: Achieve Cosmic Consciousness through selfless right actions to serve others' desires. Break bondage to action by action alone. Through repeated acts of selfless service, sever bondage and achieve liberation from action.

Serving others' desires — practicing Karma Yoga — we transcend personal limitations. Content within on the level of the Self, we feel confident and capable. Life's dualities (success and failure, ups and downs, progress and reversal, starts and stops) and the distracting fear of undesirable outcomes lose influence. Actions feel natural, purposeful and right. We enjoy performing them. The harmony between outer actions (lower self) and nonactive inner contentment (higher Self) strengthens union between the two.

Repeated acts of selflessly serving others' desires strengthen union of bounded self within unbounded Self. Optimism rules. Possibilities pop out of the woodwork. Actions feel spot on. Outcomes become more easily attained. Harmony between inner contentment and outer activity strengthens. In the groove of service, we increasingly identify with unbounded inner contentment of Self. In time, we fully identify with inner contentment. Union of bounded lower self within unbounded higher Self stabilizes. We *cast away the bondage of karma* (2.39) and become established in union, established in Yoga (following verse).

2.48. *Having abandoned attachments and become established in Yoga, perform actions balanced in success and failure, Arjuna. Balance of mind is called Yoga.*

'Established in Yoga,' established in union (previous verse).

Balance of mind arises from the equilibrium of contented higher Self. *'Established in Yoga,'* the contented higher Self permeates lower self's mental faculties of imagination, will, feelings, thoughts, and actions. Spontaneous right actions centered in cardinal virtues (2.45) dominate; potential outcomes hold little sway. Unmindful of outcomes, we inherently perform *'actions balanced in success and failure.'*

Union of finite within infinite, self within Self, cultivates balance of mind. Union is Yoga. Therefore, *'balance of mind is called Yoga.'*

Liberation from action:

2.49. *Far away from the balanced mind is action of inferior quality, Arjuna. Pity those who perform selfish actions for the fruits of action alone. Seek refuge in the intellect.*

For *'balanced mind'* see previous verse.

'Far away from the balanced mind' lose foresight, direction and focus. Allow emotional attachments to gain sway, perform feeble and ineffective actions, and fail to achieve outcomes. Fritter away life on the horizontal plane. Unmindful of action's true purpose, stumble along life's dharmic path of evolution, at best.

'Pity those who perform selfish actions for the fruits of action alone,' bound to the ever-changing phenomenal world, trapped on the rollercoaster of dualities, numbed by the inevitable ups and downs of life, and caught off balance by twisting turns of fate. So attached to success and failure in acquiring *'fruits of action alone,'* lose sight of the vertical plane and growth in spiritual wellbeing. Remain forever glued to the cycle of impression-desire-action, frustrated with lack of

evolution, stuck in disappointment, and pitiful in action and outcome. Quit the rollercoaster: act!

'Seek refuge in the intellect.' Practice Karma Yoga. Selflessly serve the desires of others. Follow dharma's compass heading (2.40). Innocently turn within through selfless action (2.45). Through the innermost cognitive function, the ego (intellect's subtlest quality), we identify with Absolute Self. In the equanimity of Self, gain balance of mind (previous verse). Perform right actions (2.47). In the fulfilling harmony uniting inner contentment and outer activity, experience inner strengths. Perform dynamic actions to further evolution and readily achieve outcomes (following verse).

2.50. *Intellect united with the Self, cast off good and evil actions even here in this world. Devote yourself to the practice of Karma Yoga* [to serving others' desires]. *Achieve skill in action.*

To dismiss them, Krishna addresses the full range of action. Good (or right) actions in accord with dharma support evolution; evil (or wrong) actions in discord with dharma retard evolution (2.47). Through good actions prosper. Through evil actions suffer. All actions lie between the outer bounds of good and evil, between outcomes of prosperity and poverty.

Through the ego, the subtlest quality of intellect, realize the ultimate Reality and Truth: I am unbounded inner contentment of Self (previous verse). '*Intellect united with Self*' through the ego, live outside time, space and the entire range of actions and their consequences. Live in the unbounded contentment of Self.

'*Devote yourself to the practice of Karma Yoga.*' '*Be without the three Gunas*' (2.45). Be without action. Break bondage to action. Let nonaction of contented Absolute Self flourish. On the level of lower self (united in Self) perform right actions (2.47). Beyond action on the level of nonactive higher Self, naturally *'casts off good and evil actions even here.'*

In Cosmic Consciousness gain *'skill in action.'* Active lower self united in nonactive higher Self, live beyond attachments and dualities of loss and gain and the fear they engender. Active lower self united in Absolute higher Self, perform spontaneous, smooth and effective right actions to further evolution. This is *'skill in action'*: lower self in union with higher Self, actions based in nonaction, actions liberated from bondage to action, actions beyond concern for outcomes and consequences, actions balanced in success and failure, actions that achieve desired outcomes.

'Skill in action' is wisdom realized in action seeded by Nature's desire to further evolution (following verse).

Wisdom:

2.51. *Having renounced desire and established intellect in the Self, the wise do not need fruits born of their actions. Liberated from the bondage of rebirth they live eternally in a state free from suffering.*

Serve others' desires and innocently renounce your own. *'Having renounced desire'* no longer search for happiness in attractive qualities found in objects of sensory experience (2.39, 2.45).

Desires renounced, attention follows dharma's compass pointing toward increased happiness experienced at finer levels of awareness. Having reached finer levels of awareness deep within, the ego identifies with unbounded contentment of

Absolute Self. Through ego, intellect establishes itself in desireless Self (2.47).

From whence desires? The intellect established in "desireless" Self, the mind operates on Nature's desires. Since Nature's desires spark actions to further evolution, all actions are right actions (2.47). We spontaneously act in accord with Nature and consequently, Nature supports our actions to achieve the greater good for all. Wise indeed.

Established in inner contentment of higher Self, *'The wise do not need fruits born of their actions'* to achieve happiness. Happiness comes from contented Self deep within (2.66). The wise still enjoy fruits of action. But in fact, *'the wise'* did not desire fruits. Desires for fruits emanated from Nature's desires to further evolution in spiritual and material wellbeing along the path to happiness and fulfilling actions (previous verse).

Rebirth means to repeat a condition, to be reborn in the same state of bondage and suffering in the cycle of impression-desire-action. Wise, *'Liberated from bondage,'* rebirth to achieve liberation in separation of higher Self from desires and actions of lower self is unnecessary.

'Liberated from the bondage of rebirth [the wise] *live eternally in a state free of suffering,'* in a state where Nature's desires spark spontaneous right actions, underscore happiness and further evolution.

2.52. *When your intellect crosses the thicket of delusion, you will be indifferent to that which is yet to be heard and to that which has been heard* [in the Vedas].

Surrender to Nature's desires (previous verse). Naturally cast away the pull of past and future to achieve happiness. Live in the present.

When the ego identifies with the unbounded Absolute Self, intellect and mind cross over the '*delusion*' of looking "out there" to some future or past event for happiness and contentment.

Fulfilled, desireless and wisely acting on Nature's desires to further evolution (previous verse), '*that which is yet to be heard and that which has been heard*' in the Vedas fails to spark interest in Vedic action. On the contrary, living in a state of wisdom where Nature's desires spark spontaneous right actions underscores happiness and furthers evolution (previous verse), '*All the Vedas are of no more use than is a small well flooded by water on every side.*' (2.46).

2.53. *When your intellect stands steadfast in the Self, disregarding Vedic doctrine, then you shall attain to Yoga.*

Your intellect '*stands steadfast in the Self*' when its subtlest quality, the ego, identifies with the ultimate Reality and Truth (2.50): I am Absolute contented Self. In uniting with higher Self, the lower self turns to higher Self (2.45), '*disregarding Vedic doctrine*' on action (previous verse). We '*attain to Yoga*' (union) and act on Nature's desires to further evolution (2.51).

2.54. Arjuna asks: *How does a man of steady intellect absorbed in the Self speak, sit and move?*

'*Intellect* [becomes] *absorbed in the Self*' when the ego — intellect's subtlest quality — identifies with unbounded Self during acts of selfless service. In earlier verses, Krishna described the underlying psychological properties of Yoga (fulfilled, virtuous, balanced, discerning, skilled, wise, indifferent to the Vedas, steadfast in the Self: 2.46 – 2.53) and raised Arjuna's curiosity about the outward appearance of a man whose intellect is *absorbed in the Self.*

How does he express himself? Do pearls of wisdom fall from his lips?

How does he appear at rest? Is his countenance peaceful?

How does he appear in action? Does he move with fluidity and grace?

There is no universal answer to these questions because it is the unique personality of the lower self that performs all actions. Given the vast diversity in outer appearances among individuals, their distinctive traits and circumstances, Krishna answers in terms of inner nature. In *steady intellect absorbed in the Self* achieved during selfless service to others — the practice of Karma Yoga — one rises above selfish desires and emotional attachments (2.55 – 2.56). In the remainder of this chapter, Krishna raises the bar above *steady intellect* and describes inner nature in terms of *established intellect* — Cosmic Consciousness — verses 2.57 – 2.71.

Steady intellect:

2.55. Krishna responds: *Having cast off desires deep within the mind, content in the Self by the Self alone, one gains steady intellect.*

When we serve others' desires, we innocently renounce our own. We *cast off desires* to find happiness in sensory experiences. The cycle of impression-desire-action begone (2.45). Desires no longer grip the mind, destabilizing it by dragging it out into the ever-changing material world promising happiness in objects of the senses.

Contentment is single-sourced to the Self, '*by the Self alone.*' The ego — the subtlest quality of intellect — identifies with contented Self. Out of equilibrium of Self's inner contentment, '*steady intellect.*' In the Transcendental Consciousness of steady intellect, inner contentment infuses feelings, thoughts and actions. Some of it sticks.

2.56. *He whose mind is free from anxiety when experiencing misfortune, whose desire for pleasures has disappeared, whose attachment to passion, fear and anger have departed, he is a sage of steady intellect.*

A sage — a wise person who acts according to Nature's Laws governing evolution — sees the desireless Self as separate from activity and acts on Nature's desires to further spiritual and material wellbeing (2.51).

In the gentle equilibrium of fulfilling inner contentment of Self (previous verse) we remain '*free from anxiety*' and unmoved by '*desire for pleasures*' gained in the material world. Strong emotions lose their grip. Content deep within, '*attachment to passion, fear and anger*' lose sway. Such is a '*sage of steady intellect,*' absorbed in the rock-solid contented nature of Absolute higher Self.

Having experienced one's inner nature, established intellect dawns out of steady intellect (following verse).

Established intellect:

2.57. *He who has no attachments, neither overly rejoicing nor deeply saddened on gaining what is pleasant or unpleasant, his intellect is established.*

'*He who has no attachments*' (previous verse).

'*His intellect is established*' who permanently identifies with unbounded, desireless, nonactive, and Absolute higher Self. Established intellect anchors the mind in the ever-full ocean of contented Self. Actions fail to make deep impressions on the mind and seed desires and actions anew (2.39). In fulfilling contentment of higher Self, objects of the senses lose their allure. '*He who has no attachments*' to objects of the senses lives in quiet inner awareness of outer experiences (2.51).

Established intellect is Cosmic Consciousness. Conscious awareness remains uninvolved with activity, both cognitive and physical. Distinctions between activities of waking, sleeping and dreaming disappear. We live in the evenness of unbounded contentment of rock-solid Self, '*neither overly rejoicing nor deeply saddened on gaining what is pleasant or unpleasant.*'

Life flows of its own accord. Ups and downs tide into each other. Thoughts and actions mesh without effort. Things get done. You are in the groove of service.

2.58. *When he completely withdraws his senses from their objects, as a tortoise withdraws limbs into its shell, his intellect is established.*

The tortoise's limbs (senses) withdraw from connecting the tortoise (mind) with the outer world of sensory experiences.

For one not established in intellect, desires drag the mind out into attractive qualities of objects sensed. On the other hand, the *'intellect established'* in the Self (previous verse), inner contentment precludes the need to find happiness in objects of the senses. No longer in demand to experience happiness, the senses lose their grip on the mind. *Sans* the senses grip, the mind is an island unto itself in a Self-same sea of contentment. It is as if *'He withdraws his senses from their objects, as a tortoise withdraws limbs into his shell.'*

2.59. *Objects of the senses turn away from those who abstain from them, but the taste for them remains. Upon seeing the Supreme Truth even this taste ceases.*

Through the senses, desires drag the mind, intellect and ego into ever-changing sensory experiences (previous verse). But when we serve others' desires — practice Karma Yoga — we naturally renounce our own desires for gaining happiness in objects of the senses.

In steady intellect gained in serving others, the mind no longer *'feeds'* upon objects of the senses through desire. For the man of steady intellect, it is as if the *'objects of the senses turn away from those who abstain from them.'* But until intellect establishes itself in the Self (2.57), *'the taste for them remains.'* That is, the objects still have their waxing and waning allure. Upon actually *'seeing the Supreme Truth'* of omnipresent Self detached from objects, *'this taste ceases.'*

Control:

2.60. *The turbulent senses forcibly carry away the mind, Arjuna, even of the astute man who strives to resist them.*

The senses fall under the control of their objects "out there" and take on their turbulent quality. Through desire, the senses connect the mind to its objects of desire (2.58). Thus, *'The turbulent senses forcibly carry away the mind, even of the astute man who strives to resist'* being caught up in their turbulence.

A discerning nature and resistance is not enough to bar being *'forcibly carried away.'* Rather, a more stable force effortlessly "controls" the senses from within (following verse).

2.61. *Having controlled the senses, disciplined, let him sit united in the Self, his attention on Me as Supreme; for he whose senses are controlled, his intellect is established.*

Established intellect brings the senses under control by outshining their alluring objects. When the ego — the subtlest quality of intellect — identifies with higher Self it becomes established in the Self (Practice makes perfect, 2.47). Thus, the lower self — ego, intellect and mind — sits *'united in the Self'* and takes on its Absolute unbounded nature.

Fulfilling inner contentment of Self outcompetes fleeting happiness "sensed" in alluring objects (2.39). Ego, intellect and mind are *'disciplined'* and *'controlled'* by inner contentment of Self, rather than the other way around where attractive qualities found in objects of the senses discipline and control mind, intellect, and ego. Through inner contentment, steady intellect and balance of mind overcome *'turbulent senses'* (previous verse).

'His attention on Me as Supreme.' Previous verses attested to the inadequacies of selfish desire and petitionary Vedic action to further evolution. [*'All the Vedas are of no more use than is a small well flooded by water on every side (2.46). 'You will be*

59

indifferent to that which is yet to be heard and to that which has been heard' [in the Vedas] (2.52). See also verses 2.42 – 2.44.] So where do we turn to gain deeper knowledge of Self? Ans: to '*Me as Supreme.*' For He alone is someone to whom the seeker can turn.

Anger:

2.62. *From pondering on objects of the senses, attachment. From attachment, desire. And desire gives rise to anger.*

Looking for happiness outside ourselves, we risk setting off the chain reaction of attachment, desire, anger. '*From pondering on objects of the senses,*' we become attached to the object's attractive qualities. '*From attachment, desire*' to experience lasting happiness the object promises. '*Desire gives rise to anger*' when our actions to find lasting happiness in the object fail to meet expectations.

2.63. *From anger arises delusion; from delusion loss of memory; from loss of memory, destruction of intellect; from destruction of intellect, he perishes.*

Anger opens the floodgates of delusion. We see our world through the lens of the false reality we create to justify angry feelings. Our delusional narrative is so wonderfully intoxicating, we disengage from harmonious rhythms of life and the steady course forward along our path of evolution.

Memory breaks loose from fact. '*From delusion loss of memory.*' We make things up to support our delusional narrative. Imagination out competes reality. The difference between what happened and what we imagine having happened confuses us on the nature of reality.

Logic and common sense whirlpool down the drain. Based on false and fanciful input and loss of memory, intellect has an unstable factual basis and dysfunctions. Properly functioning intellect discerns what is real and true. Dysfunctional intellect loses power of discernment.

'*Destruction of intellect*' leaves us adrift. Without means to correct course and steer around life's reefs, and across its shallow and stormy seas, we flounder on the hard rocks of a delusion-based ignorance. We embrace enchanting ignorance with open arms. Disaster ahead. Having abandoned life's natural rhythms, '*he perishes*' in his pursuit of higher levels of spiritual and material wellbeing.

Happiness:

2.64. *But having disengaged from desire and anger, disciplined and moving among objects of the senses, liberated from their attractions and aversions, and under his own control, he attains inner peace.*

In union, lower self takes on the contented nature of higher Self and is disciplined and controlled by it (2.61). The lower self infused with fulfilled higher Self, no need for selfish desire and consequently, no anger is born ('*desire gives rise to anger*,' 2.62).

'*Under his own control*,' that is, lower self naturally controlled by higher Self (2.61), he moves '*among the objects of the senses, liberated from their attractions and aversions*.' Liberated in the higher Self's full and unbounded nature, lower self casts away attachments, possessions and the need to possess. Having detached from stormy outside influences, '*he attains inner peace*.'

2.65. *Through inner peace comes an end to all sorrows; from inner peace the intellect steadies.*

Ending sorrow is a matter of control. Mind, intellect and ego controlled by the senses, there is always risk of sorrow from losing something dear. But the Self-controlled (2.61) run no risk of sorrow. Unbounded inner peace leaves no room for loss, sorrow, sadness, and distress induced by outside influences (previous verse). Absorbed in inner peace, intellect steadies in its role to discern our Real and True nature, which is, in fact, happiness born of peace of mind (following verse).

2.66. *No Self-control, no intellect, no steady thought, no peace of mind; for one lacking peace of mind, can there be happiness?*

This verse brings the previous two to a happy conclusion.

In union, individual aspects of lower self (ego, intellect, mind) come under the control of contented Absolute higher Self (2.61). However, lacking union, these aspects of lower self fall under the control of the '*turbulent senses*' (2.60). Lacking union of lower self within higher Self, there is '*no intellect, no steady thought, no peace of mind*' operating in their roles to steer us along our dharmic path (2.40).

There is no '*steady thought*' in minds endlessly searching for happiness and consequently, '*no peace of mind.*' '*For one lacking in peace of mind, can there be happiness?*' How can there be happiness when the mind flits about searching for it "out there?" Only when we realize inner contentment of higher Self can we achieve steady thought, peace of mind and naturally experience happiness from within.

Peace of mind comes not from overtly controlling it. Instead, by serving others' desires, we achieve peace from within by uniting lower self within higher Self (2.45), eliminating the draw of turbulent senses and their tempestuous nature to rough us up.

Withdraw senses from their objects:

2.67. *When the mind follows the wandering senses, the intellect is carried away by the senses as a ship is carried away by wind on water.*

'*The turbulent senses forcibly carry away the mind*' (2.60). When the weak mind becomes absorbed in enjoying an object's attractive qualities "out there" in the relative field of life, it loses the inclination to find lasting happiness deep within (previous verse). Regardless, the mind naturally appeals to the intellect to discern Reality and Truth in the relative, where there is neither. The higher Self loses "control" of ego, intellect and mind to the senses. The senses exert the turbulent influence of the relative on mind, intellect and ego. Consequently, as the mind is carried away by the turbulent senses '*the intellect is carried away by the senses as a ship is carried away by wind on water.*'

2.68. *Therefore, Arjuna, he whose senses withdraw from their objects, his intellect is established.*

This verse deepens the metaphor of 2.58, '*as a tortoise draws in his limbs.*' There the focus was on established intellect. Here the focus is on the end game of happiness, where '*Therefore*' takes us back to 2.66: '*how can there be happiness*?'

The senses latch onto their objects through the desire for the happiness attractive qualities found in them promise. Thus, through the mind, *'the intellect is carried away as a ship by wind on water'* (previous verse). But finding a greater source of happiness found deep within, the senses *'withdraw from their objects.'* We find this greater source of happiness only when *'his intellect is established'* in the unbounded contentment of Self, that is, in the union of lower self within higher Self, wherein reside peace of mind and resultant happiness (2.66).

Live Cosmic Consciousness:

2.69. *The Self-controlled remains awake in that which is night for all beings. On the other hand, the time in which all beings are awake is the night for the sage who sees.*

The realized and unrealized experience wakefulness differently. The realized is eternally awake in the light of the Self, experiencing separation from activity. The unrealized is awake to desire, delusion, attachments, binding influence of action, wavering intellect, and unsteady thought.

'Self-controlled' refers to verse 2.61: in union, the contented Self infuses lower self with inner contentment and in this subtle way, controls ego, intellect and mind.

The *'Self-controlled'* experiences the contented nature of the Self through the intellect established in it (2.57). The light of contentment shines through all activities, whether in states of waking, sleeping or dreaming. *'The Self-controlled remains awake* [to the contented nature of Self] *in that which is night for all beings.'* That is, when unrealized beings sleep in the night, the realized remains awake on the level of the Self.

On the other hand, the unrealized is awake to the fleeting satisfaction of objects of the senses. The sage of established intellect sees this state of bounded wakefulness as merely the darkness of ignorance. '*The time in which all beings are awake is the night for the sage who sees.*' Thus, relative to experiencing the bright light of the Self, wakefulness of the unrealized is pitch black as the darkest night '*for the sage who sees.*'

2.70. *He for whom all desires enter the mind as waters enter the full and undisturbed sea attains peace, and not he who longs for objects of desire.*

For those whose intellect is established in the Self the purpose of all desires has been achieved: union of lower self absorbed in unbounded, eternally lasting inner contentment of Absolute Self. The bright light of Self shines through the intellect, illuminating the mind. Desires are already fulfilled (2.46). '*All desires enter the mind as waters enter the full and undisturbed sea*' of inner contentment.

On the other hand, for the man '*who longs for objects of desire*' each desire is vitally important and carries the heavy burden of necessity. Happiness depends on achieving this very desire!!! The pressure is on. He sees bondage to action as the way things get done and the means to happiness. That is, bondage is a good thing. For '*he who longs for objects of desire*' is bound to his actions to experience their transient measure of happiness. Deluded, he lives in the dark night of ignorance (previous verse).

2.71. *When a man abandons all desires and acts without longing, he lives independent of the sense of 'I' and 'mine.' He attains inner peace.*

Detached from desires, '*a man abandons all desires and acts without longing*' because he — the lower self of ego, intellect, mind, senses — lives absorbed in the contented higher Self (previous verse). Desires still occur on the surface of the mind. But these are Nature's desires to further evolution (2.51) and there is no sense of '*I*' and '*mine*' associated with them. Liberated! Happiness (2.66), the purpose of all desires and actions, has been achieved (previous verse). Hence, there is nothing to long for. [See also 2.45, '*free of possessiveness, possessed of the Self.*']

2.72. *This is Cosmic Consciousness, Arjuna: freed from delusion and established in this, even in the hour of death, he attains eternal freedom in eternal happiness.*

'*This is Cosmic Consciousness*' refers to the attributes Krishna describes in verses 2.57 – 2.71.

Quiet and content deep within, we witness desires on the surface of the mind and the organs of action act. Intellect '*established in this*' inner peace of Self, we abandon desires and longing, achieve indifference to the sense of '*I*' and '*mine*' and gain 'liberation '*from delusion*' of looking "out there" for happiness in objects of the senses.

Peace of mind puts an end to anxiety, sorrows, sadness, and distress. Happiness flourishes. We experience quiet inner awareness of contented Self during waking, sleeping and dreaming. Always and forever established in the inner peace of Self, '*even in the hour of death, he attains eternal freedom in eternal happiness.*'

Chapter 3 — Experience Sacrifice of Desire

Overview of Ch 3:

Sacrificing desire is in our DNA. When we selflessly serve others' desires (Ch 2), we sacrifice our own. We trust higher powers to help us further spiritual and material evolution. Relying on Nature by acting in accord with the natural law of right actions, Nature supports us. We feel liberation fuel us forward through ups and downs, thick and thin, success and failure. How to sacrifice desire? Do your duty. Take the householder's path: serve the desires of those you honor and love. Through selfless actions in everyday life, sever attachment to objects of the senses and break bondage to action. Put your better nature in control. Quickly gain faith in your forward momentum and trust in the practice of Karma Yoga to separate Self from action. Release yourself from sinful wrong actions retarding evolution. Go with the flow of selfless service. Do your duty: sacrifice desires and the selfish actions they seed. Instantly experience harmony between lower self and higher Self. Find yourself merrily tapping a foot in tune with the groove of life. Follow the music.

Paths: 1&2 Because Krishna emphasized understanding in the previous chapter, Arjuna naturally sees the pursuit of knowledge through intellectual understanding as superior to action. But unsure of how to proceed, Arjuna asks by which path he will reach the highest good. 3 Krishna informs Arjuna about paths of contemplation (mental action) for the recluse and of action to achieve outcomes for men and women of action, the householder's path. Both paths accomplish the same goal of separation from action, that is, living in nonaction separate from action. 4 But nonaction is not achieved by abstaining from action; abstaining from action is still action. Nor does one achieve perfection in action by renunciation of action alone. Krishna's take-home message: action is the name of the game; act, be it mental along the recluse path or actions to achieve outcomes along the householder's path. But to evolve, act you must.

Action: You can run but you can't hide. 5 It is impossible to disengage from action. To survive and evolve, the Gunas of Nature — the three forces upholding action and evolution introduced in the 45th verse of Ch 2 — relentlessly drive everyone to action. 6 Restraint accomplishes the opposite of intended effect. Restraining the organs of action while dwelling on objects of the senses, kindles desire for restraint; desire for restraint seeds actions of restraint. 7 The key to nonaction on the level of the Self? Practice Karma Yoga. Engaging the organs of action without bondage to action — by selflessly serving others' desires – is the means to separate higher Self from action. Reach the highest good through the Yoga of action, practice Karma Yoga.

Do your duty: 8 Performing duty is the direct means to practicing Karma Yoga. Sacrifice selfish desires and actions they seed: '*Be without the three Gunas.*' Duty out of love and devotion comes naturally and spontaneously breaks bondage to action. Action out of duty trumps selfish action; by acting for others, we travel the path of least resistance to reach the "highest good" for all. Enhance harmony between quiet inner awareness and outer activity. Readily reach spiritual and material goals by performing your duty to others.

Sacrifice desire: 9 Duty requires sacrifice. To sacrifice desire, practice Karma Yoga and free yourself from attachments and bondage to action. 10 Sacrifice of desire was simultaneously created along with humankind. It is in our DNA and natural to perform. 11&12 Sacrifice of desire creates a mutually beneficial relationship with the subtle forces of Nature that promote evolution. By sacrificing desire, Nature rewards us with liberation. 13 Feeding on liberation resulting from sacrifice of desire, releases the righteous — those practicing Karma Yoga — from sinful wrong actions retarding evolution.

Born of Brahma: 14 Sacrifice of desire trumps petitionary Vedic acts of sacrifice and instantly starts the ball of evolution rolling. 15 All selfless acts of sacrifice are born in Brahma arising out of all possible Veda and cause only good and increase. Whenever we sacrifice desire, we sacrifice *with* Brahma, enlivening the support of Nature and furthering evolution in spiritual and material wellbeing.16 Without following our path of evolution and infusing Brahma into sacrificial actions, we live in vain. 17&18 Find delight in the higher Self alone. Self-reliant, obviate the need for others. 19. Just do your duty, truly unattached from action perform sacrificial actions. Achieve inner contentment. Find happiness within.

Perfection: 20 By action alone ancient leaders gained perfection by performing actions that supported individual and societal evolution. They acted for the welfare of others, as should you. 21 Great men set high examples of right action through sacrifice of desire for others to follow. 22 Krishna needs do nothing and yet, attains all worth attaining. 23 Men in every way follow His example: duty to the evolution of humankind. 24 If Krishna did not act, confusion would reign and absent his example, civilizations would crumble. 25 Follow Krishna's example of action without bondage. Practice Karma Yoga by serving others' desires. 26 Steadfast in acting for the welfare of others, the wise inspire others to act likewise.

Gunas act on Gunas: 27 The Gunas of Nature perform all action. Those who experience the Self separate from action know this Truth. Only the deluded think, '*I am the doer.*' 28. He who knows — through understanding and experience — the role Gunas play in action is not bound by action. On the contrary, he is liberated from action.

Free from delusion: 29 Thinking happiness lies within objects of desire and that experiencing happiness requires taking action to enjoy those objects is delusional. 30 Maintain contented Self through the practice of Karma Yoga. Achieve separation from desire and action. Free yourself from the delusion of involvement in action.

Faith: 31 Gaining faith in the practice of Karma Yoga comes quickly to those who follow Krishna's teaching. 32 Those who do not follow His teaching of selfless service in duty to others confuse themselves about the knowledge of action and separation of Self from it, sentencing themselves to ride out mindless actions on the whirligig of bondage.

Go with the flow: 33 Follow your nature. Go with the flow of dharma by practicing Karma Yoga. Restraining from actions accomplishes nothing except frustration and spiritual poverty. 34 Let not attractive qualities found in objects of the senses sway you. These are enemies besetting your path.

Be yourself: 35 Do your duty. The duty of another retards evolution and gets you nowhere. Your highest duty: evolve by performing duty to those you honor and love. Practice Karma Yoga.

Good and bad of desire: 36&37 Anger arises when desires collide, canceling the momentum of each. Desires go unfulfilled, efforts unrewarded. Evolution stalls. Desire and anger are your enemies. 38 Desires arise out of unbounded contented Self but overshadow it; attractive qualities in objects of the senses stimulate desire which foster happiness but overshadow Self. Desires nourish survival and evolution but overshadow Self. 39&40 Even the wise are vulnerable to the insatiable flame of desire. Desires overshadow wisdom, deluding the nature of uninvolved Self, fueling bondage to action.

Unite self within Self: 41&42 Put higher Self in control, enlightening intellect, mind and senses from within, overruling lower self with unbounded contentment of higher Self, short-circuiting attachment to objects and bondage to action. 43 Practice Karma Yoga. Unite bounded lower self — senses, mind and intellect — within contented and unbounded higher Self. Disconnect the senses from their objects by circumventing the need to find happiness "out there" in the material world. Slay the enemy in the form of desire. How? Follow Krishna's teaching: do your duty by sacrificing desire! Evolving to the highest levels of spiritual and material wellbeing is just that simple. Practice Karma Yoga.

Commentary on Ch 3 verses 1 - 43:

Paths:

3.01. Arjuna asks: *If you consider knowledge superior to action, then why encourage me to engage in this terrible deed of war?*

Because Lord Krishna emphasized understanding in the previous chapter, Arjuna naturally sees the pursuit of knowledge through understanding as superior to action. The notion of pursuing understanding alone gives Arjuna the hope he is on the right track and can avoid battle. Consequently, Arjuna asks, '*Why encourage me to engage in this terrible deed of war?*'

3.02. Arjuna continues: *Your opposed statements confuse my intellect. Tell me surely this one thing: how shall I reach the highest good?*

Something is missing from Krishna's teaching and Arjuna cannot put his finger on it. Intellectual understanding has been insufficient to assuage his confusion, dithering and unhappiness. Yet he cottons to the idea of ridding himself of troubling issues through understanding alone (previous verse). Stumped, he needs Krishna to distinguish between paths of contemplation and action — and set him on the right one. '*Tell me surely this one thing: how shall I reach the highest good?*'

3.03. Lord Krishna responds: *As set forth by Me in ancient times, there are two paths, Arjuna: the Yoga of pursuing knowledge for men of contemplation and Yoga of action for men of action.*

The 'Yoga of pursuing knowledge for men of contemplation' and the 'Yoga of action for men of action' were 'set forth' in ancient times by no less than Me and have withstood the test of time.

'Men of contemplation' achieve renunciation by overtly resisting desire and restraining from acting in the extroverted world of social interactions. They turn attention inward through mental activity of quiet study and contemplation — Gyan Yoga, the recluse path (3.05).

'Men of action' take action to serve others' desires, innocently renouncing their selfish desires and the actions those desires seed — Karma Yoga, the path of action, the householder's path (3.05).

Both paths accomplish the same goal: Yoga and happiness in Cosmic Consciousness (2.72).

There are no hybrid paths. The path-switching recluse strains fundamental vows of chastity and poverty. The path-switching householder strains responsibility. In either case, strain disrupts the harmonious integration of lower self within higher Self. Evolution to reaching the 'highest good' stalls.

The following two verses illustrate essential differences between practices of Gyan and Karma Yoga.

3.04. *Not from abstention from action does a man attain nonaction. And not by renunciation alone does he approach Perfection.*

Practitioners of Yoga (previous verse) cannot escape action. The 'man of contemplation' chooses mental action (Gyan Yoga). The 'man of action' chooses physical action to achieve outcomes (Karma Yoga). Both courses of action achieve union of lower self within higher Self.

'Nonaction' is the experience of Self separate from action.

'Renunciation alone' is the state of Cosmic Consciousness where the Self finds itself 'alone' and separate from desires and actions (Ch 2).

'Perfection' exceeds wisdom of Nature. Wise, we act on Nature's desires (2.51). In 'Perfection' the Divine Brahma infuses all action (3.15).

'Abstention from action' is the act of abstaining. Therefore, abstention does not achieve nonaction. Far from it. At its core, abstention is merely making a mood of nonaction and faking detached Self — and not the real deal.

And not by renunciation alone does he approach Perfection. 'Renunciation alone' is the state of Cosmic Consciousness. We live in 'renunciation alone,' in separation from everything. In time, separation from everything 'approaches perfection' (4.18).

Action:

3.05. *Indeed, not even in the twinkling of an eye can one exist without performing action. The Gunas born of Nature drive everyone to action.*

Action begins when the Gunas of Nature enliven functioning ego. At this point, the experiencer, that experienced and the process of experiencing come into being. This is the beginning of action manifesting out of pure consciousness, the unmanifest field of all possibilities. Hence, all reality — ice cream, turtles, stars, kitchen cabinets, thinking — is action born of ego born of the Gunas of Nature. [For a deeper dive into the triad of experience and God's non-transcendent and transcendent natures relationship with it, see verses 7.04 – 7.12 in Appendix 3.]

Awareness is the eternal present. There is no measure of time short enough to exclude the present and trilogy of experience. *'Indeed, not even in the twinkling of an eye can one exist without performing action.'*

By contemplating Nature's subtle laws, the Gyan Yogi transcends the most refined level of ego through revelation. Awareness of the finest level of creation cannot be achieved on the level of the ego because the act of thinking overshadows awareness of creation at a level finer than contemplation. Consequently, the Gyan Yogi can only experience the transcendental beginning of action from outside the experience trilogy. In seeing the Truth of Reality through contemplation — simultaneously realizing its transcendental and relative aspects — the Gyan Yogi transcends action through revelation. Revelation is the "aha" moment where intellectually understanding the experience trilogy merges with experience of it. Thus, the Gyan Yogi sees the Truth of the Self separate from action through revelation.

Relative to the practice of Karma Yoga, this revelatory means to transcend ego is indirect and contingent on culturing a refined nervous system. Consequently, the practice of Gyan Yoga requires a reclusive lifestyle — restrictive diet, quietude, celibacy, reliance on a master's teaching — to help settle the nervous system and support *'contemplation'* of Nature at a refined level of the mind. The reclusive lifestyle is a tough row to hoe for men and women of action (3.03).

For the Karma Yogi, transcending ego is directly accomplished through action (2.45). Anytime. Anywhere. Serve others' desires and instantly transcend your own selfish desires and the actions they seed. '*Be without the three Gunas,*' be without action by simply acting to serve others' desires and experience nonaction on the level of the Self.

3.06. *He who sits restraining his organs of action while dwelling on objects of the senses, self-deluded, he is a hypocrite.*

'*Restraining*' chooses lethargy. He chooses the horizontal plane of selfish action and numbs himself to the joys of selfless actions in service to others, accomplishment and evolution.

He who wastes precious time on restraint and dwelling is delusional. Restraint and dwelling are selfish actions — albeit mental actions — of self-control inspired by a poorly understood concept of desireless nonaction. Regardless of intention, selfish actions are actions all the same and keep us in bondage to action (2.39). Therefore, he who believes the self-delusion that '*restraining his organs of action while dwelling on objects of the senses*' achieves liberation from action is untrue to himself. Duped, he fails to practice what he preaches. '*He is a hypocrite.*'

3.07. *But he who controls the senses by the mind alone, Arjuna, and without attachment engages the organs of action in the Yoga of action, he excels.*

Yoga means union and the '*Yoga of action*' is action taken in union of lower self within higher Self (2.45). In union, the mind (of lower self) becomes infused with unbounded contentment of higher Self (2.61). In this way, the higher Self gains control of the mind, which controls the senses, which guide the organs of action to achieve outcomes. Actions based in unbounded Absolute higher Self, he gains skill in action (2.50). '*He excels.*'

Do your duty:

3.08. *Do your duty! Act! Act, for action is indeed superior to inaction. Even the maintenance of your body could not be accomplished without action.*

Q: How to engage the organs of action in the '*Yoga of action*' (previous verse)? What specific actions guarantee neither loss of effort nor obstacles to evolution (2.40). How to practice Karma Yoga and act without acting and achieve nonaction in action (2.45)? ... experience cardinal virtues blossom (2.45)? ... achieve fulfillment and render the Vedas as useless as a small well surrounded by water on every side (2.46)? ... instinctively perform right actions (2.47)? ... gain balance of mind (2.48)? ... achieve skill in action (2.50)? ... employ Nature's wisdom in all actions (2.51)? ... establish intellect in the Self (2.57, 2.58)? ... control wavering senses (2.61) ... achieve Cosmic Consciousness?

Ans: '*Do your duty!*'

Duty! In its simplicity lies its completeness. '*Men* [and women] *of action*' fulfill purpose and responsibility by taking action to meet responsibilities. Doing your duty to serve others' desires is all it takes to '*be without the three Gunas*' (2.45). The rewards of evolution in spiritual and material wellbeing require nothing more than duty.

Putting others' needs first is what we do to fulfill purpose and responsibility. We serve others' desires by sacrificing our own. To sacrifice desire is to feel liberation from action and the flow of dharma. When we pitch in, we slip into the groove of life and evolution.

To do otherwise, act selfishly or slide into inaction, feels rough and out of step with evolution. Entropy gains the upper hand and the family of man falls into dysfunction. Success in action and evolution suffer.

In sacrificing desire, men and women of action break the cycle of impression-desire-action (2.45). Self-purifying and comfortable, sacrificial actions enhance harmony between quiet inner awareness and outer activity, hastening evolution. Our good vibrations radiate to those we hold dear. Intellect steadies and readily becomes established in the Self. We spontaneously perform right actions supporting evolution. Content deep within, desires and actions take care of themselves.

This is the practice of Karma Yoga experienced through the householder's 'duty': actions out of love and devotion fulfill dharma, serve the purpose of spiritual and material evolution, and reach 'the highest good' for all, the exalted goal set by Arjuna in verse 3.02.

Take the path of least resistance. 'Act, for action is indeed superior to inaction.' Choose the vertical plane. 'Do your duty!' Meet your responsibilities. Act. Innocently sacrifice selfish desires and actions they seed. Liberate yourself from action, achieve skill in action (2.50) and readily reach spiritual and material goals.

Or choose inaction and stumble along the horizontal plane. Choose lethargy, idleness, dullness. Choose resistance, strain, indifference, and unhappiness. Choose inaction and fall in league with entropy. Get nowhere fast.

No duty, no action, no evolution to Cosmic Consciousness. *'Even the maintenance of your body could not be accomplished without action.'* Although self-evident, this sentiment underscores the notion that action is necessary to survive. Without surviving, no evolution to higher levels of spiritual and material wellbeing. Therefore, we must act to survive and evolve. The motivation to successful, sustainable and rewarding action on all levels of life? Ans: Duty!

Immediately following verses address renunciation of action through sacrifice of desire (3.09 – 3.10) and support of Nature in sacrificial actions taken (3.11 – 3.15).

Sacrifice desire:

3.09. *Aside from acts of sacrifice, this world is bound by action. Perform actions for the purpose of sacrifice, free from attachments.*

Sacrifice is an action unto itself, apart from all others and created for experiencing liberation from bondage.

Krishna uses *'bound'* in two ways. First, we are bound to act because our survival depends on it: *'Even the maintenance of your body could not be accomplished without action'* (previous verse). Second, when we look for happiness in objects of the senses — rather than sacrifice desire and find happiness within ourselves — we become bound to our actions to experience the lasting happiness those objects falsely promise (2.39).

'Perform actions for the purpose of sacrifice, free from attachments.' Make the sacrifice of desires by serving others'

desires your *raison d'etre* for acting: practice Karma Yoga in '*this world.*' When we sacrifice desire and act in service to others — a natural consequence of staying the householder's path (previous verse) — we operate on the level of contented Self and free ourselves from attachments. The Self just is, eternal, '*maintenance*' free, outside the field of action, and '*free from attachments.*'

3.10. *Having created humankind along with Sacrifice, the Lord of Creation said: "By this Sacrifice you will prosper and fulfill all desires."*

Sacrifice is an action unto itself, apart from all others (previous verse) and created by none other than the Lord of Creation for experiencing liberation from bondage, prosperity and fulfillment of desires.

Gifted by the Lord of Creation, sacrifice of desires comes naturally. Sacrifice is in our DNA. We were born to practice Karma Yoga: serve others' desires by sacrificing our own. The message is clear. By sacrificing desires, '*you will prosper and fulfill all desires.*'

But exactly how are prosperity and fulfillment of desires accomplished through sacrifice? By gaining Nature's support in all endeavors (following five verses).

3.11. *By sacrifice, you nourish the gods and the gods nourish you. By nourishing each other, you reach the highest good beneficial to all.*

Here, 'gods' are subtle forces that organize and govern the positive direction of evolution in spiritual and material wellbeing.*

Team Evolution: We share responsibility with the gods to further evolution. The gods organize subtle laws of Nature and administer refined impulses of intelligence and energy to work out the mechanics of evolution. In selfless sacrifice of desires to serve others, we engage these refined impulses, give them purpose and direction and create a reality (3.05) that furthers the spiritual and material evolution Nature presides over and the gods work out.

Gratitude ground-truths the present. Through gratitude, we nourish the gods and the gods nourish us. We put trust in gods and Nature. We hand desire and impulse over to them, optimizing their charter to support evolution and ours to carry out the actions they engender. Recognizing the god's existence and purpose through gratitude strengthens our shared bond to further evolution and in our recognition of their role, nourishes their creative powers to support our evolution.

And from our side, gratitude naturally directs attention to the present, eliminating attachment to objects of the senses and bondage to action. In the present, we feel positive, content and happy from within. To '*reach the highest good beneficial to all*' we bond with higher powers, gain skill to carry out actions and achieve the outcomes Nature supports to further evolution. Incorporating Nature's wisdom and the gods' organizational and administrative skills into our selfless actions sustains and nourishes us.

Harmony gained in working together ratchets up mutually beneficial nourishment: '*By nurturing each other, we reach the highest good beneficial to all.*' That is, together, we put our shoulders to the wheel of cosmic purpose (4.18, 4.20, 4.21).

*About '*gods*,' briefly: The First of the Ten Commandments recognizes "other gods." In this and subsequent verses, these '*gods*' are universal laws of Nature operating to further evolution. Something like, "A stitch in time saves nine," "The early bird gets the worm," "Faint heart never won fair lass," etc. These universal laws are foundational to right action and as true in the Owen Stanley Range of New Guinea as in the taco stands of Kiev. There are enumerable such laws and in daily activity it is best to acknowledge their truths and allegiance with Nature: "You can run but you can't hide." Recognizing these gods — refined laws of Nature— nurtures them in fulfilling their role to support right action and nurtures us in achieving spiritual and material wellbeing.

For more on the *Gita's* monotheistic nature and religious tolerance, see "Personal God" (verses 7.20 – 7.23) in Appendix 3.

3.12. *Brought into being by Sacrifice, the gods will truly bestow the enjoyments you desire. But he who enjoys their gifts without offering to them in return is a thief.*

This verse meets the Lord of Creation's declaration, '*By this Sacrifice you will prosper and fulfill all desires*' (3.10).

By sacrificing desire, we bring the gods into being to support Nature's purpose to further evolution (previous verse).

For men and women of action, *ex-post* offerings of gratitude win in a knockout punch over *ex-ante* petitionary offerings, that is, over petitionary prayer and Vedic offerings. Having sacrificed desire, '*The enjoyments*' you desire are, in fact, the ones Nature desires for you to further your evolution (2.51). Moreover, fulfilling Nature's desire is on the god's job description (previous verse). So, of course, '*Brought into being by Sacrifice* [of desire] *the gods will truly bestow the enjoyments you desire,*' that is, Nature desires for you to further spiritual and material evolution.

Fruits of actions are '*gifts*' from Nature and the gods and not our doing. To assume authorship of action and outcome is to deny the creative roles higher powers play. Without offering gratitude (previous verse) '*to them in return,*' we fail to provide nourishment which sustains them and us in our supportive roles to further cosmic purpose (previous verse).

A thief suffers his low level of consciousness, the worst punishment of all. Denying higher powers their due, the thief assumes authorship of desire, becomes bound to fruits of action and robs himself of the profound happiness liberation from action offers. Through thievery, he foregoes life in the present, enjoying fruits of action free from bondage, peace of mind, and happiness (2.66).

3.13. *The righteous, who eat the remainder of Sacrifice, are released from sin. But the non-righteous, who prepare food for their own sake, they eat sin.*

The remainder of sacrifice is liberation. By consuming liberation through action, we infuse the universal nature of higher Self into individual self and enhance union of self within Self. In union, lower self naturally performs selfless right action that support evolution (2.47). '*The righteous ... are released from sin.*'

The '*non-righteous*' perform selfish wrong actions to enjoy attractive qualities found in objects of the senses (2.47). They selfishly '*prepare food for their own sake.*' '*They eat sin*' born of thievery (previous verse), sentencing them to sinful wrong actions and bondage.

Born of Brahma:

3.14. *From nourishment beings manifest, from rain is produced nourishment, from Sacrifice comes forth rain and Sacrifice is brought into being by action.*

This verse and the following drill down to the nature of sacrifice. Our sacrificial actions get the ball of creation rolling (this verse) and infuse Brahma into sacrificial acts (following verse).

Sacrifice of desire trumps petitionary Vedic offerings to produce rain, nourishment and beings. Born of '*action*' in sacrificing desire, intellect established in Self (2.57). Out of established intellect, '*rain*': renewal *via* Nature facilitating evolution (2.51). Out of '*rain,*' nourishment of gratitude to sustain the gods administering the laws of Nature acted upon by the Gunas (3.11). Out of the Gunas of Nature, '*beings manifest*' through functioning ego (3.05). Clearly, '*Sacrifice*' requires action; no action, no sacrifice.

3.15. *Know all actions originate in Brahma. Brahma arises from the Imperishable. Therefore, all-pervading Brahma is eternally established in sacrifice.*

This verse and the previous drill down to the nature of sacrifice. Our sacrificial actions get the ball of creation rolling (previous verse) and infuse Brahma into those sacrificial acts (this verse).

Transcending effigy and divine status, Brahma is the creative upward-flow of increase out of the field of *all* possibilities. In embryonic form Brahma infuses *all* things that both support and retard evolution. This verse clearly states that Brahma is '*eternally established in sacrifice.*' That is, Brahma the Creator is present in all acts that sacrifice desire. To engage sacrifice of desire is to engage the primal creative force in the universe.

'*Know all actions originate in Brahma.*' Brahma the Creator is the source of all activity and therefore, infuses all activity. '*Brahma arises from the Imperishable*' unmanifest field of all possibilities (Veda) that permeates and supports life and evolution. All selfless acts of sacrifice of desire support life and evolution and are born in Brahma arising from '*the imperish*able.' Therefore, Brahma infuses sacrifice of desire and enlivens those actions sacrifice of desire seeds to further evolution in spiritual and material wellbeing. Essentially, we sacrifice *with* Brahma, not *to* Brahma, thereby easily infusing Brahma — the primal creative force — into consciousness, feelings, thoughts, and actions.

3.16. *One who does not follow the wheel set revolving, Arjuna, who performs sinful wrong actions, whose contentment lies in the senses, lives in vain.*

We propel a bicycle forward by downward and upward strokes of the pedals. Life evolves from one stage to the next, dissolving one by bringing the next into the moment. With each sacrifice of desire — each performance of duty (3.08) — we gain a more evolved state of life and in the process, destroy the previous, lesser-evolved one. Creative and destructive forces work in harmony, revolving the wheel of evolution forward along our dharmic path, maintaining balance and life moving forward.

Those who fail to perform their duty (3.08), waste precious time and energy in straining to gain forward momentum. They lose harmony and balance. They lose Brahma's establishment in sacrificial actions (previous verse), which infuses selfless action with forward momentum, harmony, balance, evolution, and support of Nature.

'*One who does not follow the wheel set revolving, who performs sinful wrong actions,*' acts selfishly. Selfish acts retard evolution (2.47). Attempting to selfishly fulfill desires by vainly looking for fulfillment in attractive qualities found in objects of the senses we become attached (2.39). Attached, we cannot '*follow the wheel set revolving.*'

'*Set revolving*': '*Brahma arises from the Imperishable*' (unmanifest field of all possibilities, previous verse). By sacrificing our desires to serve others' desires, we adopt action already set in motion. Just jump on, start peddling and '*follow the wheel* [already] *set revolving.*'

Without infusing Brahma into sacrificial actions (previous verse), we live in vain. We struggle on our own to evolve. We spin away on the cycle of impression-desire-action.

3.17. *But the man who delights in the Self alone, whose source of contentment is the Self alone, for him the need to act does not exist.*

In Self-awareness achieved by practicing Karma Yoga (2.45, 3.08), we live detached from desires and actions, in union of lower self within higher Self, experiencing contented higher Self. '*For him the need to act* [to achieve happiness and contentment in objects of the senses] *does not exist.*' Instead, happiness lies in peace of mind born of contented Self alone (2.66).

3.18. *Neither action nor inaction has any purpose. And he has no need of any living creature for any purpose whatsoever.*

'*Neither action nor inaction*' achieves happiness already realized in contented '*Self alone*' (previous verse). Happiness born of contented Absolute '*Self alone,*' does not rely on the actions of '*any living creature for any purpose whatsoever.*'

3.19. *Therefore, do your duty. Perform action truly unattached and attain the Supreme.*

'*Do your duty*' (3.08) and follow the '*wheel set revolving*' (3.16). Practice Karma Yoga and innocently sacrifice desires by serving the desires of those you are responsible for. Desires sacrificed, break bondage to action and the cycle of impression-desire-action. In this way, '*perform action truly unattached*' to desire, action and outcome. Infuse Divine Brahma's sacrificial action into yours and so, '*attain the Supreme*' Brahma in your dutiful actions (3.15).

Perfection:

3.20. *Perfection was gained by King Janaka and others by action alone. For the mere welfare of the world, you should act.*

Sacrificial actions infuse Brahma into those performing them (previous verse; 3.15). In this way, '*by* [sacrificial] *action alone*' to serve their subjects, '*King Janaka and others*' gained perfection. Content in the Self by the Self alone left no room for doubt. Attaining '*perfection*' is no more complicated than that: '*Do your duty!*' (3.08); infuse Brahma into your actions; gain unwavering contentment; gain perfection (3.15).

Krishna admonishes Arjuna to rise above selfish individuality. Even if Arjuna merely stands up, he will sacrifice desire, rise above his cowardly confusion and infuse Brahma into his actions and gain '*Perfection.*'

Keep the welfare of others in mind. '*For the mere welfare of the world, you should act*' in service to others' desires and attain '*Perfection*.' This path '*King Janaka and others*' followed '*by action alone.*'

'*Action alone*' drives home the point of previous verses in this chapter. To gain higher states of consciousness, live the highest levels of spiritual and material wellbeing, and '*reach the highest good*' you do not need Vedic text, pundits, complex systems of philosophy, religious rites, pilgrimages, recluse lifestyle, obsequious obedience to a master. To put your best foot forward, fulfill duty, nourish the gods, gain their favor, receive Nature's support, infuse Brahma into all action, follow the wheel set revolving, delight in the Self, gain perfection … all you need is '*action alone.*' Act to serve others' desires. Transcend petty individuality. Stand up. Fight! Act!

3.21. *Whatever a great man does, so do the rest; the world follows standards a great man sets.*

Set a good example. Our actions influence others. Perform actions according to the high standards exemplified by great leaders (previous verse): '*Do your duty!*' (3.08). Serve others' desires, infuse Brahma into your actions, and shine the Divine light forward (3.15). Through your good example, help put a shine on others' actions and together, create a more abundant and just world (2.60).

3.22. *For Me, Arjuna, there is no action in the three worlds I need do. Nor is there anything not attained to attain. Regardless, I engage in action.*

Having dealt with the world of men and the importance of duty to life *exemplar* in the previous verse, Lord Krishna offers himself as an example of duty. Living free from activity in the relative, '*Regardless, I engage in action.*' I do my duty in the transcendental field of the Divine to support continuity in life and evolution.

3.23. *What if I did not continue unwearied in activity? Men in every way follow My example, Arjuna.*

Duty is the highest order of action on all levels of creation. '*If I did not continue unwearied in activity?*' there would be no high example of duty to follow (previous verse). The take-home message: follow my example, '*Do your duty!*' (3.08).

3.24. *If I did not act, these worlds would perish and I would cause confusion and destroy these people.*

'*If I did not act,*' there would be no continuity in transcendent and relative fields of life. Good and increase would fail to flourish. Confusion would reign supreme. '*These worlds would perish*' in the helter-skelter of apathy and instability (3.22). The take-home message: so will your world perish if you do not perform sacrificial actions.

3.25. *While the unwise act out of bondage to action, Arjuna, so the wise should act without bondage, desiring the welfare of the world.*

Action is action and based on desire, wise or unwise.

The unwise commit their energies to the horizontal plane of survival and material gain, stuck in the cycle of impression-desire-action, living with vain hope for something better. In bondage to action, the unwise act on their selfish desires to find happiness in objects of the senses. As a result, they fail to experience contentment glow from within. Without the glow of inner contentment infusing their actions, moral and ethical values stagnate.

Attempting to navigate life with neither polestar of morals nor compass of ethics, they fail to reach the port of steady virtuous actions. Rather, in the hit-or-miss of right and wrong action, they steer to the edge of perishing into the helter-skelter of apathy and instability (previous verse).

On the other hand, the *'wise act'* on Nature's desire to further evolution (2.51) and so uplift the *'welfare of the world.'* *'The wise'* do their duty. They innocently sacrifice their own desires and consequently act on Nature's desires *'without bondage,'* achieve inner contentment and experience moral and ethical values blossom (2.45).

3.26. *The wise should not create a division in the minds of the ignorant who are bound to action. Steadfast in performing selfless actions, the wise inspire others to act likewise.*

The *'ignorant'* search to experience liberation from desires and actions. Performing selfish actions seeking recognition sends the wrong message and creates *'a division in the minds of the ignorant.'* Rather, setting an example of dutiful selfless actions shows the way (previous six verses). Acting in accord with Nature's desire (2.51), *'the wise inspire others to act likewise.'*

Gunas act on Gunas:

3.27. *The Gunas of Nature perform all actions. He whose mind is confused by egoism holds, 'I am the doer.'*

Nature sows the seed impulses to further evolution through the gods (3.11) and through the gods, *'the Gunas of Nature perform all actions.*' Only those who directly experience separation of Self from action — in either the practice of Karma Yoga ('*steady intellect,*' 2.55) or living Cosmic Consciousness in daily life ('*established intellect,*' 2.57) — know the Truth of action.

This verse is the experience equivalent of understanding gained in verse 2.71: '*Independent from the sense of I and mine.*' When we identify with contented Self (2.45), we innocently abandon egoism and the sense '*I am the doer.*'

However, '*He whose mind is confused by egoism*' and holds '*I am the doer*' lives in ignorance of the Gunas carrying out actions. He sees himself as the performer of action and the achiever of outcomes. From lack of directly experiencing detachment of Self from action, he is '*unwise*' (3.25) — that is, he has not wised up — to acting on Nature's desires (2.51).

3.28. *But he who knows the Truth about the role Gunas play, Arjuna, knowing Gunas act upon the Gunas, is not bound to actions.*

To know the Truth about the Gunas is to experience action separate from contented Self (previous verse). Absorbed in contentment, we innocently see action unfolding of its own accord. We know — through understanding and direct experience — '*the Truth about the role Gunas play.*'

Free from delusion:

3.29. *Those deluded by the Gunas of Nature are bound to the actions of the Gunas. Those who know the whole Truth should not disturb the ignorant who know only partial truth.*

The 'ignorant' search to experience liberation from desires and actions.

'Those deluded by the Gunas of Nature' do not know 'the Truth about the role Gunas play' (previous verse). In the absence of inner contentment, attractive qualities found in objects of the senses kindle desire. Thinking happiness lies within the object of desire and that happiness requires taking action to experience the object deludes the ignorant. They become 'bound to the actions of the Gunas' in cycles of impression-desire-action (2.39), thinking 'I am the doer' (3.27).

'The ignorant who know only the partial truth,' intellectually understand this 'whole truth' about the Gunas acting on the Gunas but they have not experienced liberation from action. Therefore, rather than proffer intellectual understanding alone and create confusion, one 'who knows the whole truth' about the Gunas should encourage others to take action: 'Do your duty!' Then and only then will they see the whole Truth through the experience of separation from action.

3.30. *Defer all actions to Me, maintain the Self, free yourself from selfish desire, and depart from delusion. Fight!*

Step up to the plate. Serve others' desires. 'Fight!' 'Do your duty!' (3.08). Instantly liberate yourself from 'I am the doer (3.27)' and break the bondage to action. 'Maintain the Self' separate from actions, deferring 'all actions to Me.'

Faith:

3.31. *Those who faithfully follow my teaching accept it without finding fault, they are liberated from bondage to action.*

Q: Exactly what is Krishna's teaching?

Ans: '*Do your duty!*' (3.08).

Gaining faith in this practice of Karma Yoga comes quickly. Even those new to the practice '*who faithfully follow my teaching*' — those who understand the importance of duty and perform it — find no fault because no fault exists. '*My teaching*' is the effortless, obstacle-free and rewarding path. '*They* [*those who faithfully follow my teaching*] *are liberated from bondage to action*' in the Yoga of action.

3.32. *But the complaining who do not practice my teaching, know them to be confused about knowledge, doomed, mindless and lost.*

Those who find fault with My teaching fail to practice it (previous verse). Consequently, they never gain '*knowledge*' by directly experiencing liberation. They fail to feel the Divine infuse their sacrificial actions (3.15). Instead, they are '*doomed*' to bondage (2.39). They are '*mindless*': '*The turbulent senses forcibly carry away the mind*' of those confused about knowledge (2.60). They have '*lost*' their way on the path of evolution.

Go with the flow:

3.33. *One acts according to their own nature. Even the enlightened follow their nature. What will restraint accomplish?*

This verse builds on 3.06, '*He who sits restraining his organs of action.*'

Krishna summarizes the previous four verses. Men and women of action follow their nature: performing duty, sacrificing desires, breaking bondage to action, realizing independence of Self, and experiencing Divine Nature infuse all actions.

Follow your nature. Go with the flow of dharma: practice Karma Yoga (2.40). *'Even the enlightened,'* those who experience the Self separate from desire and action, follow their nature and perform right actions supporting evolution.

For men and women of action, what can restraint — holding back, caution, control — accomplish? Serving the desires of others is in our DNA and therefore is our core nature (3.10). Restraint from serving others is akin to swimming upstream. The direction is all wrong to fulfill responsibilities duty requires. Pushing against the flow of dharma, they are *'doomed'* to bondage; *'mindless'* they ride life's rollercoaster (previous verse). Indeed, *'What will restraint accomplish*?' Ans: Confusion, stress and frustration in daily life, and spiritual poverty.

3.34. *Within the object of the senses lies its attractive and aversive qualities. Do not be swayed by these enemies besetting your path.*

The weak mind sees the potential to experience happiness in an object's attractive qualities. Through desire for happiness, they become attached to the object and the happiness it promises, reinforcing bondage to action, overshadowing the Self and retarding evolution.

The power to overshadow the Self is also true for *'aversive qualities,'* say, snakebite. Fear overshadows the steady nature of Self and we become overpowered and obsessed with consequences. As a result, we lose powers of discernment and balanced mind, degrading our ability to address the situation effectively.

'Do not be swayed by these enemies besetting your path' of dharma. Attraction and aversion excite the senses, overshadowing mind, intellect, ego, and Self, throwing us off our evolutionary path to higher spiritual and material wellbeing.

Be yourself:

3.35. *Because one can perform it, one's own duty, well performed, is superior to poorly performing the duty of another. Better is death in performing one's own duty; the duty of another brings perilous danger.*

Verse 3.08 defines duty and the importance of it for achieving liberation from bondage to action.

"Be yourself, everyone else is already taken," Oscar Wilde. One can only perform one's duty well. Men and women of action should follow their dharma, go with the flow of duty and evolve to the highest levels of spiritual and material wellbeing. Or rather, attempt to perform someone else's duty, struggle to follow their dharma, fail to achieve skill in action, waste time, advance frustration and disappointment, retard evolution and stagnate on the horizontal plane.

Rather, follow your dharma. *'Do your duty!'* Practice Karma Yoga.

'Better is death in performing one's own duty; the duty of another brings perilous danger.' Death is a respite built into cosmic purpose and necessary for evolution. After dropping the body, we take on a new one and more rapid progress in evolution is possible. The greater danger of retarding evolution lies in performing someone else's duty, disrupting the course

of evolution and flow of dharma, jamming a stick into the spokes of '*the wheel set revolving*' (3.16).

Good and bad of desire:

3.36. Arjuna asks: *What is it that impels a man to unwillingly commit sin, O Krishna, as if urged by an evil force?*

3.37. Krishna responds: *The force is desire; the force is anger. The force is born of Rajo Guna, all-consuming and most evil. Know this to be the enemy.*

Rajo Guna gives desire energy and direction to bring it to fruition. A thought rises out of pure consciousness of Self and develops into a desire, and through Rajo Guna gains forward momentum. Rajo Guna has the peddle to the metal while moderating Gunas of Sattva (steering wheel) and Tamas (brakes) sit in the backseat.

Anger arises when desires collide. The momentum of one desire butts heads with the momentum of another, disrupting the trajectory of each. Desires go unfulfilled and efforts go unrewarded.

Rajo Guna steps harder on accelerators, instigating a more permanent and severe collision. Sattva and Tamas are told under no uncertain terms to "SHUT UP." Lacking these moderating influences disrupts the natural flow and harmony required to bring desires to fruition. We forfeit the objects of desire, peace of mind and consequently, happiness (2.66). Happiness lost, frustration and anger blindly set in to find it.

Frustration and anger become '*all-consuming.*' Attention flows outward to find happiness in the wreckage of desires. Lower self dominates. We lose cardinal virtues (2.45) and ethical guidance. Unchecked, evil actions hold sway. Life suffers.

How to attenuate anger? *'Do your duty!'* Establish intellect in the Self. Achieve union and experience separation of Self from desires and the actions they seed. Outsource desires to Nature and actions to the Gunas (3.11, 3.12). Perform actions in accord with evolution, where all desires seek the same outcome of happiness, travel trajectories steered by all three Gunas and are less likely to collide.

3.38. *As smoke covers fire, dust covers a mirror, as the amnion envelops the embryo, so that covers this.*

'That covers this.' Desire covers higher Self. Desire is *'the enemy here on earth'* (previous verse). Yet, desire is all important to driving life and evolution.

1) *'As smoke covers fire.'* Desires arise from pure consciousness of Self but overshadow it.

2) *'As dust covers a mirror.'* Outer attractive and aversive qualities found in objects of the senses stimulate desire — and evolution — but overshadows Self.

3) *'As the amnion envelops the embryo.'* The amnion nourishes the embryo. Desires nourish survival and evolution but overshadow Self.

Desires overshadow the uninvolved nature of Self, leaving us with the delusion that desire and action involve us. The Truth: Nature's desire furthers evolution (2.51) and the Gunas act upon the Gunas (3.28).

3.39. *Arjuna, this insatiable flame of desire veils wisdom and is the eternal enemy of the wise.*

Having realized the Self as separate from desires, we outsource desires to Nature (2.51). Yet, even then, selfish desires arise that overshadow the Self (previous verse). Such is the power of attractive (and aversive) qualities found in objects of the senses to knock us off balance.

We lose the spontaneous wisdom to follow Nature's desires (2.51) when our selfish desires overshadow the uninvolved nature of Self. Consequently, we lose wisdom when 'this insatiable flame [of selfish] desire' to experience happiness in an object's attractive qualities overshadows the uninvolved inner contentment of higher Self and Nature's role to further evolution.

3.40. *Senses, mind and intellect are said to be its domain. Through them desires overpower wisdom, deluding the dweller in the body.*

'*Its*' refers to desire which is '*the eternal enemy of the wise*' (previous verse).

In its tendency to find greater happiness, the mind shifts to the delights of imagination, overshadowing the uninvolved nature of the contented Self (3.38) and overpowering wisdom (previous verse). It is as if active imagination, which knows no limits, sucks the individualized nature of the Self — '*dweller in the body*' — out into the relative, empowering the relative *via* turbulent senses (2.60) to lord over its Absolute nature.

Unite self within Self:

3.41. *Therefore, Arjuna, subdue the senses to shake off this evil that destroys wisdom and power of discernment.*

'*Desire veils wisdom and is the eternal enemy of the wise*' (3.39).

Desire '*is all consuming and most evil*' (3.37).

The highest '*power of discernment*' arises from the intellect established in the Self (2.57).

Through desire, the senses attach mind and intellect to their objects. On the other hand, subdued senses — achieved by performing duty — surrender intellect and mind to Absolute Self. Putting the Self in "control," the senses no longer enslave mind and intellect through the office of desire (2.61). Senses subdued by performing duty, we '*shake off this evil* [of desire] *that destroys wisdom and power of discernment.*'

3.42. *They say the senses are superior. Yet the mind is superior to the senses. Moreover, the intellect is superior to the mind. That which is superior to the intellect is Self.*

A superior aspect of subjective reality incorporates an inferior one. The senses are superior to the objects they gather information on. The mind processes information gathered by the senses and is superior to senses. The intellect makes decisions on the information rendered by the mind and is superior to mind. The Self is superior to intellect and all the previous subjective aspects of lower self and Absolutely controls them through its contented Absolute nature (2.61).

When lower self unites within higher Self — when we achieve Yoga — lower self takes on qualities of higher Self (following verse).

3.43. *Having known the Self which is beyond intellect, still the self by the Self alone; slay the enemy in the form of desire, difficult to conquer.*

"Cooler heads prevail." Practice Karma Yoga by performing duty (3.08); unite bounded lower self within unbounded higher Self in daily activity (2.45). In union, the lower self — senses, mind and intellect (previous verse) — takes on the Absolute quality of higher Self. '*Still the self by the Self alone.*'

When we identify with the '*Self which is beyond intellect,*' the lower self unites with it (2.45). In union, the unbounded inner contentment of higher Self outshines happiness promised by objects of the senses, subduing desire and its hold on mind and intellect (previous three verses). Thus, we '*slay the enemy in the form of desire, difficult to conquer.*'

This is the experience of Cosmic Consciousness in daily life, performing duty by sacrificing desires. Acting on Nature's desires, feelings, thoughts and actions integrate to achieve the highest good for all. Judgments align with Nature's desire to further evolution. Divine intelligence infuses right actions. We witness ourselves moving through life along our path of evolution. We enjoy the fruits of action while unattached to them. We feel Nature's support and find ourselves going with the flow. In the groove of duty, unattached and unbounded, dynamically active and purposeful, others follow our example.

Chapter 4 — Cosmic Consciousness — Understanding + Experience

Overview of Ch 4:

Knowledge evolves from understanding renunciation (Ch 2) and experiencing sacrifice of desire (Ch 3). Understanding provides the foundation for experience to spring into verification of separation of Self from action. The familiar feeling of quiet contentment within while engaged in dynamic outer activity verifies experience. Understanding and experience ratchet up each other. Through increased verification, feelings of familiarity born of liberation of Self evolve into the experience of separation of Self from this and that. Disconnected experiences of separation quickly unite into a pervasive vision of Oneness in everything. We see Brahman's Oneness in all; we feel familiar with all; we know all. We live in the present beyond consequences of actions. We cast away doubt. Understanding and experience meld. Knowledge reigns.

Know the Supreme Secret: 1 – 3 Great leaders practiced Karma Yoga in ancient times. Direct experience validated its effectiveness by bringing order to individual life and society. But due to the passage of time, the practice was lost. Chapters 2 and 3 revealed the understanding and experience of the practice. Knowing the Supreme Secret of the practice hides in the only place you will never think to look. Right in front of your eyes.

Evolve on the vertical plane: 4 – 6 Different stuff makes up Arjuna and Krishna. Arjuna is relative, born of flesh, experiences time pass, and for him, brain chemistry drives memory. Krishna is Absolute and unchanging, manifests out of His power of creation and lives in the present. Memory not required. 7 Krishna flows into the ebb of ignorance and restores knowledge by reviving the practice of Karma Yoga. 8 Krishna protects the righteous and destroys the sinful as the practice gains a foothold in society. Societal and individual dharma evolves on the vertical plane of life.

Approach Krishna: Your dharma is to practice Karma Yoga. 9 We move along our path toward Krishna by acting in service to others. Knowing Krishna's divine birth by firsthand knowledge of liberation from time, space and causation, we reach the goal of all action. Necessity for rebirth ceases. 10 Higher Self liberated from attachment, fear and anger; purified by separation from action; and depending on Krishna's knowledge guiding our evolution, we attain His Being. 11 In taking the initiative to sacrifice desire we move toward Krishna. He instantly rewards us with liberation from action and evolution in spiritual and material wellbeing.

Know Krishna: 12 Through sacrificial actions, rewards come quickly *via* the Gunas acting upon the Gunas. 13 Though Krishna empowered the interaction among Gunas to move us forward along our dharmic path, Krishna is not involved in action. 14 Neither is He bound by action nor has He desire for the fruit of action. Liberated from action, we know Krishna's status as the eternal non-doer. 15 Perform acts of selfless service as was practiced in ancient times and liberate yourself from action. Know Krishna from His point of view of non-doing.

Know action: 16&17 Action and reaction are manifold, indecipherable and confuse even the wise. Know action from outside action; separate from action, know action depends solely on the Gunas of Nature acting to further evolution.

Separate from action, free yourself from committing sinful wrong actions that retard evolution.

See Oneness of Brahman: 18 Seeing unifying Oneness of Brahman pervading all, we see nonaction in action and action in nonaction. Relative action is full of Brahman; transcendental nonaction is full of Brahman. In its essential nature, everything is Oneness of Brahman. 19 This knowledge of Oneness — revealed through understanding and direct experience — consumes action. This and that are the same as is the difference between them. All is one. 20 One with fruits of action, we need not act to enjoy their essence, which is Oneness. 21 The same stuff makes up heart and mind: Oneness. Neither betrays the other in sinful acts that retard evolution. 22 In seeing Oneness in all, transcend dualities, gain balance, bid bondage to actions goodbye. 23 Dissolve actions and their consequences.

Sacrifice desire: Brahman infuses all actions, sacrificial actions most of all. 24 The practice of Karma Yoga is the direct means to sacrificing desire and seeing Brahman's Oneness in separate sacrificial actions of offering, oblation and fire. 25 – 30 "Offering" desire and the consuming "fire" of knowledge are common among acts that sacrifice desire. Only acts of "oblation" differ among them. 31 Out of sacrificial acts, the sweet nectar of familiarity with all. 32 All sacrifice of desire is born of action.

Take the direct path: 33 Seeing Oneness in all, feel familiar with all, know all. Direct sacrifice of desire through the practice of Karma Yoga supersedes (all other) indirect means to achieve knowledge.

Others will teach you: 34 Through humble submission, inquiry and service we sacrifice desire to those who sacrifice desire to teach us knowledge through sacrifice of desire. Out of pervasive sacrifice, Brahman.

Know the Truth: 35 Knowing the Truth of Brahman's Oneness in all, we never again fall into delusion. In seeing pervasive Oneness on all levels, we see all beings in the Self. 36 Seeing this and knowing actions as separate from higher Self, cross over all sinfulness. 37 Live in the present. 38 Clear vision. Achieve complete knowledge in the Self.

Clouds of ignorance begone: 39 Devote yourself to the pursuit of knowledge by devoting yourself to sacrificing desire through service to others. 40 Lacking knowledge and faith and of a doubting nature, we wander about in the delusion of bondage to action. Happiness remains elusive. 41 Possessed of Self and acting without doubt, cast away the binding influence of action. 42 Swing the sword of knowledge by serving others' desires and cutting away doubt that abides in the heart. The heart listens to the language of feeling. Act in service to others. See Brahman's Oneness in all. "Feel" that warm and comfy familiarity with all. Out of familiarity with all, know all. Blow away the clouds of ignorance. How? Act in service to others. Practice Karma Yoga.

Commentary on Ch 4 verses 1 - 42:

Know the Supreme Secret:

4.01. Lord Krishna: *I proclaimed this imperishable Yoga to Vivaswat, Vivaswat communicated it to Manu; Manu imparted it to Ikshwaku.*

4.02. *Received in succession, one generation to the next, the royal sages knew this Yoga. With the long lapse of time here on earth, knowledge of this Yoga was lost, Arjuna.*

4.03. *The Supreme Secret of this ancient Yoga, I have affirmed to you today because you are My devotee and friend.*

'*I have affirmed to you today*' the understanding (Ch 2) and experience (Ch 3) of this '*imperishable Yoga.*'

Where could this '*Supreme Secret of this ancient Yoga*' remain so deeply hidden it takes Divine intervention to reveal? Under a rock in a Himalayan cave? Is it embedded within a Gregorian Chant? Is it encoded in your popup toaster's warranty? What about within the conundrum of Quantum Mechanics? In the stacks of the Bodleian Library? In *Principia Mathematica*?

None of these. Grouse around long enough and you will find it.

The only place to secret away this '*imperishable Yoga*' is in the only place you would never think to look. Ans: Right in front of your eyes. It is just too common to notice.

When dharma prevailed through Krishna's practice of Karma Yoga, right actions became natural in daily activity. Selflessly serving others' was spontaneous, fulfilling and unfortunately, too obvious for its own preservation. Hence in time, the ancients took the practice of Karma Yoga for granted. There was nothing particularly noteworthy about right actions when widely practiced.

'*With the long lapse of time*' the ancients lost the knowledge of how sacrificing desire transcends the relative and fuels evolution in spiritual and material wellbeing. Without understanding, the experience of sacrificing desire lost its scaffolding and its uniqueness among all actions went unnoticed.

Selfishness in daily life held sway. Material gain through selfish actions eclipsed the subtleties of inner contentment, peace of mind and happiness (2.42 – 2.44). The ancients lost the synergy between understanding and experience so important to evolution. They forgot the power of gratitude and its importance to living in the present and nourishing higher powers — and themselves. They assumed authorship of action and outcome. They overpowered Nature's natural flow in their busy presumptive egoism.

Selfish wrong actions replaced selfless right actions. The ancients lost the primal importance of duty. Adharma prevailed.

The Supreme Secret of '*this ancient Yoga*' to revive dharma and right action through the practice of Karma Yoga? Ans: Follow Krishna's teaching, '*Do your duty!*' Sacrifice desire for the desires of others. Achieve liberation from action. Feel at home in the world.

Evolve on the vertical plane:

4.04. Arjuna asks: *Your birth was later, the birth of Vivaswat came earlier. How can I understand that You proclaimed it in the beginning?*

4.05. *Krishna responds: Many births have passed for you and for Me, Arjuna. I know them all but you do not.*

4.06. *Although I am birthless and my nature is imperishable, I am Lord of all beings and manifest through my own power.*

Arjuna and Krishna are made of different stuff. Arjuna is relative. He has been reincarnated into different forms innumerable times. Arjuna's memory is a function of brain chemistry and is based on what he has experienced in this incarnation. Arjuna experiences through lower self, subject to limited vision and far beyond recalling all he has been — let alone what he had for lunch yesterday. He is what he is.

On the other hand, Krishna is made of sterner stuff. He is not so much born as created out of his Divine nature. He is immortal and never changing. His relative nature is Absolute. Birthless, he lives in the present he creates. He is always the same and indifferent to the passage of time and the need for memory. He Is what He Is.

4.07. *Whenever Dharma falls into decay and adharma gains favor, Arjuna, I manifest Myself.*

Our dharma is to practice Karma Yoga (2.40). Dharma is the omnipresent magnetic field of happiness flowing toward more fulfilling levels of spiritual and material wellbeing. Whenever we go with the flow of dharma, our path manifests in front of us. The practice of Karma Yoga is a direct means to achieve the summit of evolution: to practice Karma Yoga is to open the path and step forward along it. This intimate working relationship between practice and path brings fulfillment to life (2.46).

'*Whenever dharma* [the practice of Karma Yoga] *falls into decay*' the knowledge of selfless sacrifice of desire is '*lost to the world.*' Forward momentum along the path tapers off.

Selfish actions overshadow selfless actions in accord with dharma.

To regain natural balance in individual life and society, '*I manifest Myself*' to teach the importance of duty (following verse).

4.08. *From age to age I take birth to reestablish dharma firmly, protect the righteous and destroy those who commit sinful wrong actions.*

Selfless sacrifice of desire sets '*dharma*' back on track (previous verse). '*The righteous*' naturally perform right actions. Society spontaneously practices Karma Yoga, fulfills natural duty, reclaims cardinal virtues, and fosters growth in spiritual and material wellbeing. Such righteous actions prove increasingly valuable to society, overriding pervasive, negative influences of adharma.

'*Those who commit sinful wrong actions*' sow the seeds of their destruction. They perform selfish wrong actions in the names of material gain and power, and undermine the spiritual foundation of material wellbeing (2.42 – 2.44). When those who commit '*sinful wrong actions*' hold the reins of power and broadly influence culture, adharma flourishes. In such times lacking spiritual authority of action, wrong actions beget increasingly harmful wrong actions. Deteriorating society goosesteps down the road to disaster.

Through their selfless actions, the righteous sacrifice desire, gradually enliven Brahma in societal acts (3.15) and '*reestablish dharma firmly.*'

This '*Supreme Secret*' (4.03) of selfless right action peeks through the clouds of ignorance, steadily reestablishing cardinal virtues and balance. The righteous who act on Nature's desire to further evolution again prevail. Right actions gain momentum.

As the darkness of adharma gives way to the light of knowledge (this chapter), the wicked fall from power. The rewards of selfish wrong actions wane compared to those achieved through righteous behavior, burning up selfish desire and consequently, sacrificing the need for wrong actions and those who practice them.

Self-destruction too: There's a notion that if a lie is told often enough it will be taken as true. To some degree that's correct. But that's not the point. Rather, the perpetrator of lies comes to believe their own lies. And when reality rolls around — by definition, it always does — scaffolding drops out from under the liar. The wicked help destroy themselves. It takes time.

Approach Krishna:

4.09. *He who knows the Truth of My Divine birth and actions, leaving the body he is not reborn. He comes to Me, Arjuna.*

To '*know*' the truth of His '*Divine birth and actions*,' we must have firsthand knowledge of liberation from time, space and causation (this chapter). When liberated from the relative field of life, birth and death are out of the question. We share eternal life with Krishna. '*He comes to me*,' the source of eternal continuity.

4.10. *Liberated from attachment, fear and anger, absorbed in Me, depending on Me, purified by the austerity of knowledge, many have attained My Being.*

Desire is the culprit and the root cause of 'attachment, fear and anger.' [Desire is also necessary for life and evolution (3.38).]

Attachment: through desire, attractive qualities found in objects of the senses draw attention to the happiness promised "out there" in the relative field of life (2.39).

Fear: fear of failure is born of desiring success in the duality of success and failure (2.45, 2.47).

Anger: anger arises from colliding desires (2.62 - 2.63, 3.37).

No desire, no attachment, no fear, no anger. Hence, sacrificing desire by serving others' desires liberates from 'attachment, fear and anger.' The liberated mind becomes absorbed in fulfilling contentment of higher Self (2.46), 'absorbed in Me' as transcendent. 'Depending on Me' reminds Arjuna of Krishna's Supreme Knowledge and the importance of His teaching. [See also verse 2.61. 'Me as Supreme.' For He alone is someone to whom the seeker can turn.]

Austerity: In higher Self we live austere to worldly pleasures of lower self. 'Purified by the austerity of knowledge' we know 'the Truth about the role Gunas play, knowing Gunas act upon the Gunas' (3.28). Knowing this Truth, we naturally experience the Self separate from the worldly pleasures we enjoy on the surface of the mind.

[As we shall soon see (4.18 – 4.42), complete knowledge is based on seeing Oneness in all and becoming familiar with all. In full knowledge we live austere to doubting nature, consequence of action, committing sin, possessions, and in fact, to all doing (4.13).]

Through the practice of Karma Yoga — sacrificing desire by serving others' desires — 'many have attained My Being.' Having gained Cosmic Consciousness and jumped the hurdle of bondage to action, 'He comes to me.' He naturally and quickly evolves to union with Me as a matter of course (previous verse; 4.13). 'Many' reinforces the notion that spiritual evolution is open to all and achievable (2.40).

4.11. *As men approach Me, so do I reward them; men everywhere, Arjuna, follow My path.*

'Men approach me.' We take the initiative. In choosing to sacrifice desire, we step closer to His Being by liberating ourselves from 'attachment, fear and anger' (previous verse) and so, through growth in consciousness, 'approach Me.'

'I reward them.' 'My path' is purification gained through austerity; we travel down the path of austerity by increasing separation between Absolute higher Self and indulgent lower self (previous verse). As we approach Him, separation widens. His Being of complete separation dawns.

'Men everywhere follow My path' by naturally traveling toward the ultimate peace of mind ('happiness,' 2.66), which can only exist in complete separation from indulgent lower self. That is, we take the path of austerity to Austerity. ['My path' is duty in service to others (3.08, 3.31), the practice of Karma Yoga. 'Men' perform duty. Hence, 'men everywhere follow My path.']

Know Krishna:

4.12. *Desiring fulfillment of action here on earth, make offerings to the gods. Through sacrificial action, success comes quickly in the world of men.*

'*Make offerings to the gods*' means to show them gratitude; gratitude nurtures the gods — and us (3.11). '*Brought into being by Sacrifice* [of desire], *the gods will truly bestow the enjoyment you desire* (3.12). That is, '*Through sacrificial action, success comes quickly in the world of men.*'

4.13. *I created the fourfold order according to the shared roles of the Gunas and their pairings. Although I authored all this, know Me to be the eternal non-doer.*

'*All this*' refers to the '*fourfold order*' and relative existence created by it.

Gunas create *via* the '*fourfold order.*' Fourfold refers to the four ways the three Gunas pair. The three Gunas can pair in six ways. But two do not support progressive development and evolution: 1) Sattva dominates Tamas and 2) Tamas dominates Sattva. Suffice to say, all action manifests from '*the fourfold order*' to create only good which supports evolution ['*Brahma arises from the* imperishable' unmanifest pure consciousness (3.15).]

'*Although I authored* [empowered] *all this, know me to be the eternal non-doer.*' The Gunas of Nature created '*all this,*' not Me. By combining their different unchangeable qualities, the Gunas initiate change and creation via the '*fourfold order.*'

Non-doing is the highest austerity. '*Know Me to be the eternal non-doer*' is an invitation to '*attain my Being*' through the austerity of knowledge (4.10).

4.14. *Actions do not leave an impression on Me; I have no desire for the fruits of action. Thus, he who knows Me is not bound by action.*

'*Know me to be the non-doer*' and therefore, I take no actions ('*though I empower them,*' previous verse). Hence, '*Actions do not leave an impression on Me*' and engender future actions.

I need nothing; I am '*the eternal non-doer*'; I did not desire any of '*this*' (previous verse). Hence, '*I have no desire for the fruits of action.*'

'*Thus, he who knows me*' as the non-doer has firsthand knowledge of non-doing. He has achieved the highest austerity and lives eternally in fulfilling contentment (previous verse). Like Me, he '*is not bound by action.*'

4.15. *Knowing this, the ancients seeking relief, performed action; therefore, perform actions as the ancients earlier performed them.*

'*Knowing this*' refers to knowing actions do not involve Me (previous verse) through understanding and experience.

'*Seeking relief*' means seeking liberation from bondage to action (previous verse).

'*The ancients*' refers back to Vivaswat, Manu and Ikshwaku, etc. in verse 4.01.

The ancients performed Karma Yoga, which '*I have affirmed to you today*' (4.03). They did their duty by sacrificing desire, liberating themselves from '*attachment, fear and anger*' (4.10). The ancients followed My path of austerity (4.10), separated higher Absolute Self from the indulgent lower self. I rewarded them with the high austerity of non-doing (4.13) and eternal contentment in My Being (4.10).

By '*therefore, perform actions as the ancients earlier performed them,*' Krishna offers a concrete example of right action and its 'rewards' (4.11), and He implores Arjuna to follow the example set by 'the ancients.' [See verses 3.20 – 3.25 for the importance of example.] The ancients fulfilled their duty, performed skillful and dynamic right actions by serving their subjects, and consequently, success came quickly to them (4.12). Having become absorbed in Me, they achieved the state of non-doing (4.13), beyond desire for fruits of action (previous verse). Freed from bondage, they know Me and share my austere experience of non-doing in eternal contentment (previous verse).

The take-home message: act as did the ancients. Practice Karma Yoga.

Know action:

4.16. *What is action? What is nonaction? Even the wise are confused in these matters. Action I will explain to you, knowing which you will be freed from committing sin.*

4.17. *One should know the nature of action. Wrong action and nonaction should be known also. Unfathomable is the course of action.*

Krishna has consistently beseeched Arjuna to act. But action, nonaction, the nature of action, wrong action, and the course of action as they relate to 'committing sin' continue to confuse Arjuna. Krishna tells Arjuna not to worry about it and so deepen his despair, 'Even the wise are confused in these matters.'

Only within the context of knowledge can the field of action be fully valued and integrated into duty. In the remaining verses of this chapter, 'I will explain to you' the knowledge which has heretofore not been addressed. With this blessing of complete knowledge, Arjuna 'will be freed from committing sin' and consequently, finally be freed from confusion and inaction. Only in knowledge — and only then — will he be able to act 'freed from committing sin.'

'Unfathomable is the course of action' lays to waste the notion of knowing courses of action as either "good karma" or "bad karma."

See Oneness of Brahman:

4.18. *He who sees nonaction in action and action in nonaction is wise among men. He is a Yogi. He has accomplished all actions.*

This verse and the following five verify experiences as we evolve along the continuum of the vertical plane of life to higher states of consciousness.

Brahman is the all-encompassing essence of the universe and exists in all things. Brahman is the cause of all change; Brahman fulfills change; yet, Brahman does not change. Brahman is the all-pervasive Golden Glue that holds all together in the Oneness of Brahman.

'*He who sees nonaction in action and action in nonaction*' sees the unifying Oneness of Brahman pervading all. Oneness of Brahman permeates everything; everything is Oneness. Action is full; nonaction is full. Relative is full; transcendent is full. All is full. All is One. And '*he who* [actually] *sees*' this has the undeniable visual experience of Brahman's Oneness.

Cosmic purpose informs wisdom; wisdom informs action. Verse 2.51 defined wisdom as acting on Nature's desire to further evolution. Here, wisdom born of seeing Oneness informs action to achieve cosmic purpose. We take on cosmic responsibility, a responsibility we are finally justified in taking and capable of fulfilling.

'*He* [who actually sees Oneness in all] *is a Yogi.*' Yoga means union. This Yogi has united nonaction and action. '*He has accomplished all action.*' Understanding (Ch 2) and experience (Ch 3) reach their confluence. They merge into Oneness of familiarity and knowledge of all (4.33).

4.19. *He who has eliminated desire and incentive from all undertakings, his action consumed in the fire of knowledge, him the knowers of Reality call wise.*

'*Desire and incentive,*' heart and mind, feelings and thoughts.

When Cosmic Consciousness dawned, desires and incentives occurred on the surface of the mind; deep within, desires and incentives no longer occurred in the Absolute nature of Self. This separation is still true. But now, Oneness composes the one hand of desires and incentives and the other hand fullness of Self. They are separate and one-and-the-same.

This knowledge of Oneness — '*in action sees nonaction and in nonaction sees action*' (previous verse) — has consumed action into nonaction. Metaphorically, action implies going from point A to point B. But points A and B are the same, that is, the same Oneness; fullness fills the two and consequently, the gap between them. No action required.

Knowing all action has been accomplished through direct experience of fullness, cosmic purpose guides the '*wise*' (previous verse), not desire and incentive for more. '*His action has been consumed in the fire of knowledge*' of fullness.

Wisdom itself guides action. *'Knowers of Reality call wise'* those who see Oneness in all and act on that experience alone to achieve cosmic purpose.

4.20. *Having abandoned attachment to fruits of action, fulfilled, independent, even when engaged in action he does not act at all.*

Previously, we *'abandoned attachment'* through feelings of inner contentment rendered by renouncing (Ch 2) and sacrificing (Ch 3) desires. As Cosmic Consciousness blossoms, we feel fulfilled in Oneness as expressed in verse 4.18: *'in action sees nonaction and in nonaction sees action.'* In seeing Oneness in all, we are One with fruits; we *'abandon attachment'* to them in our familiarity with them.

Fulfilled in seeing Oneness in all, we depend on nothing to achieve fulfillment. *'Incentive'* plays no role in action (previous verse). Instead, the organs of action act to accomplish cosmic purpose. The *'fire of knowledge'* has consumed all action to achieve happiness promised in fruits (previous verse). 'I am those fruits and those fruits are me.' Independence from possessing fruits, actions and attachments are achieved in familiarity of Oneness.

4.21. *Performing actions by the body alone, his heart and mind disciplined, having abandoned motive for possessions, he incurs no sin.*

Having *'eliminated desire and incentive from all undertakings'* (4.19), we *'abandon motive.'*

Seeing Oneness in all we become familiar with all (previous verse). Already possessing all, through familiarity with all, how can there be motivation to possess? Rather, we abandon all *'motive for possessions.'*

United in Oneness of familiarity, *'heart and mind disciplined'* in achieving cosmic purpose (4.18), neither betray the other in motivating sinful acts. Having abandoned desire, incentive and motive, *'he incurs no sin'* by performing actions by the body alone.

4.22. *Content with whatever comes his way, transcending dualities, free from envy, balanced in success and failure, in actions he is not bound.*

In seeing Oneness in all, he transcends all dualities: progress and reversal, ups and downs, easy and difficult, success and failure. He sees that all composed of dualities as One. He identifies with Oneness in all; he has all; there is nothing others have that he does not. Envy loses footing. Equanimity in Oneness and *'content with whatever comes his way'* balances success and failure. Therefore, he is not bound to success or failure or any outcome through his actions.

4.23. *Freed from attachment, liberated, balanced, acting for the sake of sacrifice, his action is wholly dissolved.*

The previous five verses addressed *'freed from attachment, liberated, balanced.'* *'Acting for the sake of sacrifice'* to achieve cosmic purpose — with neither desire nor incentive nor motivation for possession — *'the body alone'* carries out action, exonerating one from incurring sin.

'His action' itself fulfills, leaving no impression of dissatisfaction to seed desire and action anew (2.39).

Liberated from the cycle of impression-desire-action, '*his action is wholly dissolved,*' as is its consequence.

Sacrifice desire:

4.24. *Brahman is the offering. Brahman is the oblation poured out of Brahman into the fire that is Brahman. Brahman is realized by him who sees Brahman in all action.*

"Sacrifice of desire isn't only everything, it's the only thing," take on Henry Russel's quote, "Winning is the only thing."

'*Offering*': that which is most precious to sustaining life, evolution, and daily living: desire (3.38).

'*Oblation*': means for letting go of the offering; the means for sacrificing desire; the different natures of sacrificial acts.

'*Fire*': attachment to offering consumed in the fire of knowledge. [Knowledge is defined in verse 4.33.]

'*Brahman*': Brahman causes all to exist; Brahman is the pervasive and eternal Truth unifying all reality; Brahman is in everything; Brahman is now; Brahman is the Golden Glue of it all; Brahman is the Oneness we see in all diversity (4.18).

In practicing Karma Yoga, desire, serving others' desires and breaking the cycle of impression-desire-action are respectively separate actions composing 1) offering, 2) oblation and 3) fire.

But Brahman infuses all actions. Consequently, Brahman infuses action of offering, action of oblation and action of fire. Karma Yoga is the direct means to sacrificing desire and seeing Oneness in its 1) offering (of desire), 2) oblation (serving others' desires) and 3) fire (breaking bondage to action). In this way, the practice of Karma Yoga, with Oneness infusing its three aspects, is the great opportunity to gain complete knowledge by seeing Oneness and gaining familiarity with all.

Following verses (4.25 - 4.30) illustrate lesser variations on Yoga of action. '*Offering*' and '*fire*' — desire and consuming attachment born of it — are common to all sacrificial actions considered here. Variations differ only in '*oblation*,' that is, differ only in the means for sacrificing desire.

"Seeing is believing," Thomas Fuller, quote completed in verse 4.33. '*Brahman is realized by him who sees Brahman in all action.*' [See also verse 4.18.] Once seen, we realize Brahman, no going back. We see Oneness of Brahman in everything, opening the door to familiarity with all, knowledge of all and as promised by Krishna in 4.16, freedom from '*committing* sin,' Arjuna's nexus of suffering, or so he thinks.

4.25. *Some yogis perform sacrifice to the gods and others offer sacrifice by sacrifice itself into the fire of Brahman.*

'*Some yogis perform sacrifice to the gods.*' Performing sacrifice invokes acts of gratitude. Gratitude lets go of desires to achieve happiness and contentment in the material world. The refined quality of gratitude draws attention inwards to refined levels of awareness where, finally, attention is consumed in the Self. The same is true for '*others by offering sacrifice into the fire that is Brahman.*' Through seeing Oneness in Brahman, we let go of desire and '*the fire that is Brahman*' consumes it.

4.26. *Some offer oblation as hearing and other senses in the fires of control; some others offer sound and other objects of senses into the fires of senses.*

Gandharva Veda replicates the rhythms of Nature. The soothing melodies of Gandharva balance the senses and restore inner peace. In listening to the rhythms of Nature our attention turns inward; we follow the mind's natural tendency to find happiness within and we experience refined levels of awareness. These melodic *'fires of control'* sacrifice attachment to turbulent senses and let go of worldly desires that draw attention outward.

'Some others offer sound ... into the fires of senses' refers to the actions musicians take in performing music that restores balance. Putting attention on producing natural rhythms in tune with Nature, they let go of worldly desires *'into the fires of the senses.'* Their organs of action operate on the level of Nature. Their attention turns within toward refined levels of awareness.

'Other objects of senses': taste (spices, herbs, ayurvedic diet), smell (aromatherapy), sight (light therapy; architecture; abstract art), and touch (massage, oils) also restore inner peace and balance by letting go of worldly desires.

4.27. Still others offer activities of the senses and of the vital-breath in the fire of Yoga, which is self-control kindled by knowledge.'

'Which is self-control kindled by knowledge.' A life of character leads to a life of virtue. When we understand universal Truths — for example, the 10 Commandments — we act in righteous ways to incorporate those Truths into our lives. We let go of desire for lesser modes of behavior and the worldly pleasures they seek. *'Self-control'* in following understanding of righteousness guides our actions toward the greater good of a

universal Truth. [Re Asanas: What can be more fulfilling than the first sign of stretch? Letting go of that stretch.]

'*Others offer the activities of the senses and vital-breath in the fire of Yoga.*' Through natural right actions (right actions obviate, that is, consume, wrong actions; 2.47) taken in pursuit of Truth, they burn up wrong actions and lesser intentions '*in the fire of Yoga.*' Truth illuminates what the senses experience in Oneness and thus, infuses strength into '*life-breath*' seeking it, letting go of desire and torching it.

4.28. *Some offer as sacrifice their material possessions, by austerity and by the practice of Yoga. While other aesthetics of severe vows offer study of the scriptures and knowledge.*

'*Offer sacrifice as their material possessions*' means to give away possessions to the deserving. Material possessions point attention outwards toward the world of relative change and sensual pleasure. The mind freed from possessions follows its natural tendency for greater happiness, lets go of desires and turns within toward more refined levels of awareness on the level of the Self.

Here, '*by austerity*' means to sacrifice grosser levels of activity which are part and parcel of living in the material world. '*By austerity*' we let go of desire, purify the body, integrate physical and mental systems, and operate at more refined levels. [Also see verses 4.10 – 4.13]

'*By the practice of Yoga*' means taking actions that fail to register deep impressions on the mind. By breaking the cycle of impression-desire-action we let go of desire. The contented higher Self naturally draws attention inward, achieving steadiness and inner peace.

By '*other aesthetics of severe vows offer study of the scriptures and knowledge*' means to sacrifice lesser activities in the material world and put attention on the study of Nature through scripture. Through the mental activity of intellectually understanding how the *Gunas act upon the Gunas* (3.28) at the most refined levels of Nature, '*aesthetics of severe vows*' torch desire.

4.29. *Others, pour the inward breath into the outward and the outward breath into the inward, restraining the paths of inhalation and exhalation.*

The action of alternatively breathing through one nostril and the other naturally focuses attention on the inward and outward flow of breath. At the gap between breaths, when we release from '*restraining the paths of inhalation and exhalation,*' we let go of desire, our attention frees itself from action and in its relaxed state, naturally falls back on the Self.

4.30. *Yet others, who have restricted their foods, offer breaths into breaths. All these know sacrifice, and through sacrifice, they cast away sins.*

Restricting foods means restricting intake. We have less to process. Metabolism slows. The nervous system settles down. Breathing refines. We let go of desire. Attention turns within. All who perform these sacrificial acts ('*all these*' of the previous verses) direct attention toward living in the present. In the present, we let go of desires, the past dissolves and we cast away all sins from past actions — '*his action is wholly dissolved*' (4.23) — into the '*fire*' of knowledge (4.24).

4.31. *Enjoying the nectar, which is remains of sacrifice, they reach primal Brahman. This world is not for him who offers no sacrifice, how then other worlds hereafter?*

Sacrificial acts of offering, oblation and fire (4.24) leave the practitioner with the sweet feeling of familiarity from seeing Oneness of Brahman in all. This *'remains of sacrifice'* — that is, familiarity with all — verifies the practice and guides the practitioner toward *'the eternal Brahman.'*

This world offers the means — sacrifice of desire (3.09, 3.10) — to enjoy the sweet nectar of familiarity. Those who *'offer no sacrifice'* of desire in *'this world'* fail to *'reach* [familiarity with all and] *the primal Brahman.'* They fail to feel at home in this world. How can they feel at home in worlds to come?

4.32. *Sacrifices of many kinds achieve Brahman. Know all sacrifice to be born of action. Knowing this you will find liberation.*

The act of sacrificing desire is oblation. *'Sacrifices* [oblations] *are of many kinds,'* to include those sketched in verses 4.25 – 4.30. *'Know all sacrifice to be born of action,'* that is know them all born of Brahman, the root cause of action (4.18). *'Knowing this* [by understanding and experiencing Oneness of Brahman in all creation] *you will find liberation.'* That is, to achieve liberation all Arjuna needs to do is serve others' desires: Stand up! Fight! The path of liberation to seeing Oneness of Brahman is just that easily traveled.

Take the direct path:

4.33. *Sacrifice of knowledge is superior to sacrifice through material means, Arjuna. All actions, without exception, increase knowledge.*

"Seeing is believing, but feeling is the truth," Thomas Fuller, quote completed from verse 4.24.

See verses 4.18 – 4.22 for seeing Brahman's Oneness in all.

'*Knowledge*': Seeing Oneness of Brahman in all, we feel familiar with all, we know all.

The oblation for '*sacrifice* [of desire] *through material means*' requires action to settle the mind and relinquish desire through oblation. Oblation through '*material means*' is a multistep process (4.25 - 4.30): physical and mental actions inform physiology, which in turn informs psychology to settle the mind, which in turn relinquishes desire. The process must be error-free at every step. In addition, the execution and effectiveness of the action depend on expertise and amenable conditions to the action performed. Know-how is essential; timing and location must be considered. For example, expertly performing breathing exercises (4.29) at the dinner table would be difficult, rude, ineffective, and unlikely to relinquish desires — and bad for digestion.

"Fortune favors the bold." — *Latin proverb*. Sacrifice desire directly. In the practice of Karma Yoga (4.24), '*Sacrifice of knowledge*' is sacrifice that directly leads to knowledge. You cannot do two things at once. In the instant you serve others' desires you sacrifice your own. Completely. It is an infallible, one-step process to relinquish desire, anytime and anywhere. Sacrificing desire is part of the human condition: everyone is an expert (4.10).

'*All actions, without exception, increase knowledge.*' Brahman is the root cause of all action (previous verse). Consequently, Brahman pervades all actions. Therefore, all actions advance seeing Brahman's Oneness in all (4.18), feeling familiar with all (4.31) and knowing all (this verse).

Others will teach you:

4.34. *Know this! Through humble submission, inquiry and service, the knowing ones who perceive the Truth of Reality will teach you knowledge.*

'*Knowledge*' was defined in the previous verse.

'*The Truth of Reality*' is seeing Oneness in all reality.

'*The knowing ones who perceive the Truth of Reality*' see Brahman's Oneness in all creation. Familiar with all, they know all.

By '*humble submission, inquiry and service*' we sacrifice our desire for worldly pleasures to serve those who sacrifice desire to teach others sacrifice of desire. '*All actions, without exception, increase knowledge* (previous verse),' sacrificial actions more so (3.15). For those who sacrifice desire by performing actions to serve others' desires, '*The knowing ones*' will manifest along his or her path of evolution. For example, Veda Vyasa, the author of the Bhagavad Gita, has already manifested along your path.

Know the Truth:

4.35. *Knowing this, you will never again fall into delusion, Arjuna; by that knowledge you will see all beings in your Self and also in Me.*

'*Knowledge*' was defined in verse 4.33.

'*Knowing this*,' seeing the Truth of Brahman's Oneness in all with your own eyes, you will no longer fall into the delusion of seeing reality as partitioned, disorganized, incomplete, and dystopic. Rather, you will see Brahman's unifying Oneness in your Self and all creation, shredding your delusions about creation and the '*Truth of Reality*' (previous verse).

4.36. *Even if you were the most sinful of all sinners, you will cross over all sinfulness by the boat of knowledge alone.*

'*Knowledge*' was defined in 4.33.

'*Sinful*' actions retard evolution for all (2.47). Bad *juju*.

By '*boat of knowledge alone*' means that we require only knowledge to '*cross over all sinfulness*' — neither penance, pardon, forgiveness, jail time, self-flagellation, nor sympathy useful.

Feelings guide sense. Past actions make perfect sense in feelings of familiarity born of seeing Oneness in all. Living in the present, what is is supposed to be! Living wholly in the present and '*enjoying the nectar*' of feeling familiar with all (4.31), the past feels right. We feel at home. It just makes sense.

Delight sustains itself. Feelings of being at home obviate making hash of past actions through common sense, logic and reasoning. We delight from having crossed '*over all sinfulness*' by '*the boat of knowledge*' to the glory of knowledge. And that is enough! Through feeling familiar with all, it all just makes sense.

Seen in a more scientific light, we experience a current event — the present — as if all past events lead directly to it. That is, our history perfectly defines the present. Analogous to the phenomena of Delayed Choice in Quantum Mechanics, we "overwrite" the neurocircuitry of past events and create a new personal history. As if reversing roles in cause and effect, the present (effect) delineates the past (cause).

4.37. *As fire reduces wood to ashes, the fire of knowledge reduces all actions to ashes.*

'*Knowledge*' was defined in 4.33.

Brahman causes all action. Seeing Brahman's Oneness in all instantly dispenses with notions of cause-and-effect and the consequence of action. '*The fire of knowledge reduces all actions to ashes.*' We live in the eternal present of Self. Consequence of action begone.

4.38. *There is no purifier equal to knowledge. In this world, he who is perfected in Yoga, in time, finds that knowledge in the Self.*

'*Knowledge*' was defined in 4.33.

Purification clears vision. Knowledge purifies by dissolving past actions and the consequences of actions we take (previous two verses); '*his action is wholly dissolved*' (4.23). We live in the present; we experience the present unfettered by past and future.

'*Perfected in Yoga,*' perfected in union, perfected in vision. The Oneness of Brahman unifies with Absolute Self. We achieve unqualified certainty: "I am that; thou art that; all this is that" reveals itself. In feeling familiar with all, it all makes sense (4.36).

Clouds of ignorance begone:

4.39. *He who is possessed of faith gains knowledge. Devoted to the pursuit of knowledge, senses subdued, having attained knowledge, swiftly he attains Supreme Peace.*

'*Knowledge*' was defined in 4.33.

One '*who is possessed of faith*' has achieved unqualified certainty of Oneness pervading all creation (previous verse). Out of faith, expansion of heart and intimate feeling of familiarity with all. Out of feeling familiar with all, one attains knowledge of all (4.33).

Devoted to duty, '*devoted to the pursuit of knowledge.*' '*All actions, without exception, increase knowledge,*' sacrificial actions more so (4.33). By devotion to duty, we devote ourselves to sacrificial actions (3.08). Actively pursuing knowledge through sacrificial actions synchronizes heart (feelings) and mind (logic), subduing distractions born of the senses with a singular purpose of heart and mind.

'*Knowledge*' of all leaves no wiggle room for doubt (of heart) and delusion (of mind). Liberated from doubt of eternal contentment and delusion about unity of life, heart and mind harmoniously work together (also 4.21). Heart and mind simultaneously pulling oars of feelings and logic, '*Swiftly he attains Supreme Peace*' (in Brahman Consciousness, 5.29).

4.40. *The man without knowledge, who lacks faith and of a doubting nature, is lost. Neither this world nor any other nor happiness is for him who doubts.*

'*Knowledge*' was defined in 4.33.

From a '*doubting nature*,' lack of faith; from lack of faith, lack of knowledge (previous two verses). But doubt is not the problem. Instead, the problem is failing to see Oneness of Brahman in all creation (4.18 - 4.24).

Therefore, dispel doubt by devotion to duty and the pursuit of knowledge; as knowledge dawns, vision clarifies (previous two verses). See your way forward. See Oneness in all. Gain unqualified faith in the unified nature of reality (4.34) and leave no room for doubt.

'*The man without knowledge, who lacks faith and of a doubting nature, is lost.*' Without starting the practice of Karma Yoga, one naturally remains uncertain about the power of knowledge to dispel their '*doubting nature*.' Lacking the transformative experiences of sacrificing desire and of faith in the brighter future service to others renders, he remains blissfully stuck in the ignorance of attachment. In bondage to action, he is a willing servant to the dark forces of adharma (4.07). In disharmony with Nature, '*Neither this world nor that beyond nor happiness is for him who doubts.*'

4.41. *Him actions do not bind who has renounced action through the practice of Yoga, whose doubt is cut away by knowledge, who is possessed of the Self.*

'*Knowledge*' was defined in verse 4.33.

Through the practice of Karma Yoga, we renounce action (2.45). We see ourselves separate from action (Ch 2 and 3). Engaging in actions while separate from actions, in time we see '*nonaction in action and action in nonaction*' (4.18). We see unifying Brahman permeating all. We see — actually have the visual experience of — Oneness in all; we gain familiarity with all ('*nectar*,' 4.31); we know all (4.33). This knowledge of all cuts away doubt about the unified nature of reality (previous three verses).

'*Possessed of the Self*' in unified Oneness with all creation there is nothing to gain from action; in Oneness with all, we have intimate familiarity with whatever actions might gain. Nothing more can be gained by possessing the ephemeral reality of fruit! We have reached the goal of practicing Karma Yoga set by Krishna in verse 2.39. We have '*cast away the bondage of karma*,' the bondage to action. '*Him actions do not bind.*'

4.42. *Swing the sword of knowledge and cut away this doubt born of ignorance which abides in the heart. Resort to Yoga! Stand up, Arjuna!*

'*Knowledge*' was defined in verse 4.33.

"What matters most is how well you walk through the fire," Charles Bukowski. '*Swing the sword of knowledge*' means to practice Karma Yoga, the Yoga of action. Krishna invokes the image of the warrior in action He wants Arjuna's mind's eye to see. Krishna does not, in fact, instruct Arjuna to swing a sword but to '*Stand up.*' In so doing, Arjuna practices Karma Yoga by swinging the sword of knowledge born of action in serving others' desires.

'*Cut away this doubt born of ignorance which abides in the heart.*' The heart listens to the language of feeling. Ignorance sings the sweet and comfy song of inertia. On the other hand, seeing Oneness in all, we gain the intimate feeling of familiarity with all. Out of feeling familiar with all, we gain knowledge of eternal contentment and unifying Oneness

131

which underlie all action, leaving no room for doubt born of inertia.

'*Swing the sword.*' '*Resort to Yoga* [of action]. *Stand up!*' Cross over all sinfulness by the boat of knowledge alone (4.37). Purified by knowledge, dissolve actions and their consequences (4.38). Swiftly attain Supreme Peace (4.39). Dispel doubt by the pursuit of knowledge (4.40). In union with all, free yourself from the bondage to action (previous verse). Act and free yourself from sinfulness, consequence of action, dithering, doubt, and bondage to action.

All Arjuna — and you — must do is '*Stand up!*' The practice of Karma Yoga — swinging the sword of knowledge — is just that simple. Do your duty, act in service to others in even the simplest way. Gain knowledge of all. '*Stand up.*' It is just that simple.

Appendix 1: Brahman Consciousness — See Oneness in Everything

Overview of Ch 5:

See Brahman's Oneness in all. Experience calmness separate Self from action. Attain peace of mind.

Two paths: 1 Something is missing in Arjuna's comprehension of Krishna's teaching. Is the Yoga of action the means to renunciation or is renunciation the means to the Yoga of action? Which is superior, the path of renunciation for the recluse order or the path for men and women of action? Before Arjuna can proceed, he needs a definitive answer.

Take the path of action: 2 Both paths lead to the same goal of '*highest happiness*.' But to get there, the Yoga of action is superior to overt renunciation of action along the recluse path. 3 Step off the whirligig of impression-desire-action. Through the practice of Karma Yoga gain indifference to success and failure, progress and reversal, hot and cold, and all dualities of life. In liberation from action, gain freedom from bondage to action, all the while performing dynamic actions to achieve outcomes supporting evolution.

Quickly attain Brahman: 4&5 Paths of contemplation and action reach the same goals of renunciation from action and '*highest happiness*.' 6 But without the practice of Karma Yoga, renunciation of action is difficult to attain. Dedicated to the practice, quickly see Oneness of Brahman in all action. Join Brahman in complete renunciation of action. 7 Higher Self identified with Brahman, master the lower self. Live beyond action.

Act in accord with Brahman: 8&9 Seeing Oneness of Brahman in all action, enhance separation between lower self and higher Self. Spontaneously maintain the sense, '*I do not act at all.*' 10 In this nonaction of higher Self separate from action, act in accord with Brahman's separation from action. Live untouched by sinful wrong actions and their consequences.

Infuse Brahman: Perform actions for self-purification. 11 Through action, expose lower self in union with higher Self to seeing Oneness in Brahman. Infuse body, mind and intellect with Oneness. Rid lower self of elements foreign to achieving cosmic purpose. Enjoy creation fully. 12 Purified of elements opposing evolution, abandon attachments to fruits of action. Attain inner peace. The undisciplined remain attached to fruits, bound to actions spurred by selfish desire.

Create happiness:13 The mind simultaneously links the actor with action and with nonactive higher Self. Even when engaged in actions, the purified mind finds itself as Self, a silent witness to activity, resting in happiness '*neither acting nor causing action.*' 14 Out of unbounded Self, the Gunas of Nature carry out action. Experiencer, experienced and experiencing manifest out of ego. The "experiencing" component of the trinity, links action and its fruits. "Experiencing" is always in the present. This link is the happiness of the moment joining experiencer and experienced and is of Nature's doing. The Lord of Creation remains uninvolved, as do we on the level of the Self. 15. In addition to neither authoring nor creating action, the Creator remains indifferent to the consequence of action. Those ignorant of the Creators independence from action and consequence remain deluded by the nature of action and reaction.

Create Oneness: See oneness of Brahman in all action, destroy ignorance of action. 16 Seeing Oneness backlighting all reveals Brahman in all, illuminating the truth about the transcendent. 17 We create the Oneness we see in everything, which is goodness in all creation. In cause and effect, we join Brahman and go to the end of rebirth.

Achieve evenness of vision:18 In the equanimity of Brahman, we see Brahman in all things, regardless of how the Gunas act upon the Gunas. 19 Seeing Brahman in all things, the Self fully renounces action, leaving action to Nature and the Gunas. We master life by witnessing it evolve through Nature's doing. 20 Establishment in Brahman liberates us from the delusion of duality by seeing evenness in all things. Emotions moderate. Intellect steadies. We know Brahman by intellectually understanding Brahman's infusion into creation and seeing Brahman in all. 21 In this evenness of vision lies the eternal happiness we enjoy *with* Brahman.

Attenuate agitation: 22 Pleasures born of contact with objects of the senses source pain. Established in Brahman and experiencing evenness, we naturally disregard seeking pleasures in objects of the senses. 23 Seeing evenness in all things, unmoved by external sensations, and happy in evenness seen, agitation born of desire and anger attenuates.

See the transcendent: 24 Seeing the light of Brahman's Oneness in all creation, content and happy within, and finding eternal freedom from action in Brahman, we attain Brahman and fully renounce action. 25 Renouncing all action, eliminates sinful acts. In addition, "seeing" the transcendent dispels doubts about the separation of Self from action. We delight in the welfare of all beings. 26 Disciplined by Self that has attained renunciation and having cast away desire and anger, freedom of Brahman exists in all things.

Attain Peace: 27 Established in Brahman: all actions renounced, external contacts abandoned, the flow of consciousness settled on our spiritual center, and steadiness of inhalation and exhalation. Brahman's evenness fills senses, mind, intellect, ego, and the entire universe. 28 Senses, mind, intellect, and ego controlled by evenness, we achieve eternal liberation in renunciation. 29 Calmness separates Self from action. Acting in the function of Brahman, we attain peace in the form of Brahman.

Commentary on Ch 5 verses 1 – 29:

Two paths:

5.01. Arjuna: *On the one hand, You praise renunciation of action and on the other, You praise the Yoga of action. Tell me definitively, which one is better of the two?*

In this verse, '*renunciation of action*' means removing oneself from worldly life by following the recluse path of contemplation (3.03 – 3.05).

'*Yoga of action*' means the practice of Karma Yoga, innocently renouncing desire and the action it seeds by following the path of action, the householder's path of serving others' desires (3.03 – 3.05).

Before proceeding in Krishna's teachings, Arjuna asks, '*Tell me definitively* [Arjuna has asked for direction before but now gets specific], *which of the two is better?*'

Take the path of action:

5.02. Lord Krishna: *Both the renunciation of action and the Yoga of action lead to the highest happiness. Of the two, however, the Yoga of action is superior to renunciation of action.*

Here, '*superior*' means most direct and efficient to achieve the '*highest happiness*' (4.33).

A man of action (Vedavyasa) wrote the *Bhagavad Gita* about a man of action (Arjuna) for people of action (you). People of action are the true custodians of the knowledge of action (4.33). Confused about the effectiveness of either renunciation or action, Arjuna turns to Krishna for guidance.

In response to '*Tell me definitively,*' (previous verse) Krishna responds, '*The Yoga of action is superior to renunciation of action.*' In the Yoga of action — the practice of Karma Yoga (2.45, 3.08) — we renounce desire and action when we serve others' desires, instantly achieving inner '*highest happiness*' and setting our feet directly on the path to '*peace*' in Brahman Consciousness (this chapter).

5.03. *Know him to be the man of renunciation who neither hates nor covets, who remains eternally indifferent to the pairs of opposites, Arjuna. He is easily released from bondage.*

In this verse, '*renunciation*' is the state of higher Self separate from action. The bright light of '*highest happiness*' (previous verse) reigns supreme, yielding natural indifference to success and failure, pleasure and pain, progress and reversal and other dualities in the relative field of life. Lesser emotions of hate and covetousness pale in the light of '*highest happiness*' and fail to incentivize desire and action and the cycle of impression-desire-action. '*He is easily released from bondage* [to action].'

Quickly attain Brahman:

5.04. *The naïve, not the wise, declare Samkhya and the Yoga of action differ. Practiced correctly, either finds the fruit of both.*

5.05. *Followers of Samkhya and the Yoga of action reach the same goal. Samkhya and the Yoga of action are one. He who sees this, truly sees.*

'*Samkhya*' is a philosophy that brings the knowledge of separation between higher Self and action. In this verse,

'*Samkhya*' refers to study and contemplation along the recluse path of overt renunciation from action.

The '*Yoga of action*' is Karma Yoga and is practiced by those who take the path of action. In Karma Yoga, our actions serve others and in this way, we renounce our own actions (2.45).

Regardless of the path taken, reclusive or active, '*either finds the fruit of both*,' which is the '*highest happiness*' (5.02).

Samkhya and the Yoga of action reach renunciation of action through action alone, be it mental contemplation or physical action to serve others' desires, respectively.

'*He who sees*' the Oneness of Brahman in all reality (4.18) — from galaxies to quarks; from desires to thoughts to philosophies; in all diverse action — sees that '*Samkhya and the Yoga of action are one.*' '*He who sees this* [underlying reality of Oneness of Brahman pervading Samkhya and Karma Yoga], *truly sees.*'

In summary, Samkhya and Karma Yoga are '*one*' in at least five ways: 1) both sacrifice desire; 2) both are paths of liberation; 3) they reach the same goal of '*highest happiness*,' 4) both require action, 5) having reached the goal of Brahman by either path, the practitioner "sees" each in the same light of Oneness; sees one in the light of the other.

5.06. *Renunciation is difficult to attain without the Yoga of action, Arjuna. The wise devoted to the Yoga of action quickly attains Brahman.*

In this verse, '*renunciation*' means the state of detachment of higher Self from all action.

The '*Yoga of action*' is Karma Yoga and is practiced by those who take the path of action. In Karma Yoga, we serve others' desires and so, instantly renounce our selfish desires and the actions they seed.

'*The wise devoted to the Yoga of action*' quickly see Oneness of Brahman in all reality because the practice itself is the direct means of gaining renunciation (4.33, 5.02). That is, serve others' desires and naturally renounce your own. In addition, the act of service purifies the mind to where we can actually "see" Oneness of Brahman in all (following verse).

5.07. *Devoted to the Yoga of action, purified, having mastered the self, whose senses are conquered, whose self has become the Self of all beings, he is beyond all action.*

'*Devoted to the Yoga of action*' we see Oneness of Brahman in all creation (previous verse).

'*Purified*': To purify is to rid the mind of foreign elements that block seeing Brahman's Oneness in all. Purified, we see Oneness of Brahman in all; we see only the elemental good and increase in all. [See also verse 4.10, '*Purified by the austerity of knowledge.*']

'*Mastered the self*': The lower self is individuality. Seeing Oneness of Brahman in all, lower self gains universality of Oneness. In this way, universality masters individuality. [See also verse 2.61, "the lower self — ego, intellect and mind — sits '*united in the Self*' and takes on its Absolute unbounded nature." Also in 2.64, "The lower self infused with fulfilled higher Self."]

'*Whose senses are conquered.*' The senses detect unique aspects of their objects which distinguish them from other objects: a duck is not a quark. In seeing Oneness of Brahman in all, unique aspects remain, but within each — backlighting each, if you will — is the underlying Oneness of Brahman.

Seeing Oneness among unique objects conquers their uniqueness and the senses that detect them. [See also verse 2.61, 'Having controlled the senses.']

'Whose self has become the Self of all beings': the higher Self is unbounded universality, which is found in all reality, including 'beings.' The lower self in union with unbounded universal higher Self takes on the qualities of Oneness higher Self identifies within 'all beings.' In this way, lower self becomes the Self of all beings. [See also verse 4.35, 'by that knowledge you will see all beings in your Self and also in Me.']

'He is beyond all action' whose Self identifies with Oneness of Brahman and like Brahman, is not involved in action at all. Enjoying the fullness of Brahman, which is increase of happiness, we do not feel the need to act to achieve happiness in objects of the senses.

Act in accord with Brahman:

5.08. *Seeing the Truth of Brahman, he maintains 'I do not act at all,' whether seeing, hearing, touching, smelling, tasting, walking, sleeping, breathing.*

5.09. *Talking, moving, letting go, grasping, opening and closing the eyes, he believes the senses abide in objects of the senses.*

Verses 5.08 and 5.09 address passively and actively experiencing separation of Self from action, that is, experiencing renunciation from action.

Separation of Self from action initially retains some residue of attachment. Upon gaining Cosmic Consciousness we feel unfamiliar with this experience of higher Self separate from action because the observation itself lies in the field of action. And action overshadows the Divine nature of separation.

Seeing Oneness of Brahman in all enhances separation between Self and action and clinches the feeling of familiarity with it. The Self "sees" its independence from action. The experience component of knowledge catches up with the understanding component. The quiet knowledge '*I do not act at all*' reveals itself (5.08).

In this state of Brahman-level nonattachment, the senses and organs of actions act of their own accord. We realize Divine separation and live the axiomatic truth that '*the senses abide in the objects of the senses.*' All that "out there" — whether passively or actively experienced — is not of our doing whatsoever. We live separate from that.

5.10. *Acting in accord with Brahman, having abandoned attachments, his acts are untainted by sin as a lotus leaf by water.*

Though a lotus flower floats in water, the essential nature of its watery environment rolls off its leaves without wetting them.

Living separate from all relative (previous verse), we abandon attachments to objects of the senses. We act in accord with Brahman to achieve cosmic purpose (4.18). Even though emersed in a world of sinful incentives, acts that retard evolution fail to impress the mind and lead to sinful acts. '*His acts are untouched by sin as a lotus leaf by water.*'

Infuse Brahman:

5.11. *With the body, mind and intellect and even by the senses alone, Yogis perform action for self-purification, having abandoned attachment.*

Yogis live separately from action (5.08 – 5.10). Actions remain on the level of body, mind and intellect. Since *'the senses are conquered'* by Brahman (5.07), they corporally function with fruits of action independently of higher Self.

Activity is essential for *'self-purification.'* Engaging lower self in activity when seeing Oneness in all, infuses Oneness into body, mind and intellect of lower self ['*Mastered the self*,' 5.07]. Infusion purifies lower self, ridding it of elements foreign to seeing Brahman's good and increase in all action (5.07).

5.12. *Disciplined in the Yoga of action, having abandoned the fruit of action, he attains inner peace. The undisciplined ones remain attached to fruits of action, bound to actions spurred by desire.*

'Disciplined in the Yoga of action [the practice of Karma Yoga],' he acts *'for self-purification'* (previous verse). *'Having abandoned fruits of action'* and the vicissitudes of the relative field of life, *'he attains inner peace'* of Absolute higher Self. [See also verse 2.64, "Having detached from stormy outside influences, *'he attains inner peace.'*"]

'The undisciplined ones' *'act* [not] *for self-purification.'* In the absence of *'inner peace,'* they seek pleasure in fruits of action. They *'remain attached to fruits of action, bound to actions spurred by desire,'* stuck in the cycle of impression-desire-action (2.39).

Create happiness:

5.13. *Renouncing all actions with the mind, the dweller in the body rests in happiness, in the city of nine gates, not acting at all, nor causing action.*

The '*city of nine gates*' refers to the human body: two eyes, two nostrils, two ears, the mouth, and the organs of excretion and generation.

The mind's capacity to simultaneously maintain action and nonaction links the actor with action and with nonactive higher Self. Having become as familiar with higher Self as with action, the mind sustains nonactive higher Self when engaged in action. In this way, contented higher Self protects the mind from attachment to action. No attachment to action, action '*renounced.*'

'*Renouncing all actions with the mind,*' that is, '*having abandoned the fruit of action, he attains inner peace*' (previous verse). [From verse 2.66, '*For one lacking peace of mind, can there be happiness?*'] Having gained '*inner peace*' (previous verse), '*the dweller in the body* [the individualized nature of the Self] *rests in happiness … not acting at all, nor causing action,*' separate from action.

5.14 *The Lord does not create either the authorship of action or the action of people. Neither does the Lord create the link between action and its fruits. Nature carries this out.*

The mind links outer and inner (previous verse). Simultaneous activity on the surface of the mind and nonaction of unbounded Self deep within the mind compose life. Out of the unbounded pure consciousness of Self, the Gunas of Nature create action, where experiencer (actor performing '*action*'), experienced ('*fruit*') and experiencing come into being through functioning ego (3.05). Nature creates '*the link between the action and its fruits*,' the '*link*' being the "experiencing" component of the experience trio.

In Cosmic Consciousness, this '*link between the action and its fruits*' is happiness. '*The dweller in the body rests in happiness* (previous verse).' '*Rests*' accurately describes experiencing happiness linking '*action and its fruits*,' a refreshing repose of least activity authored by the Gunas of Nature.

The Lord stands indifferent to authoring action, fruits of action and the link of happiness between the two. '*Nature carries this out*' via functioning ego (3.05).

5.15. *The Lord recognizes neither sinful nor virtuous deeds of anyone. This wisdom of indifference is veiled by ignorance. By ignorance people are deluded.*

So, in addition to indifference to authoring action and to linking action and its fruits ('*happiness*,' previous verse), the Lord remains aloof to the experience of action, whether sinful or virtuous. The Gunas of Nature carry out all action and all experience of action (previous verse). The Lord remains a silent witness to action and experiencing, whether sinful or virtuous.

The ignorant are unaware of this separation between the Lord and action. Thinking the Lord grants fruits of action and runs a complex accounting system for leveling reaction, rewards and retribution deludes them. This delusion obscures independence from actions and the trilogy of experience carried out by the Gunas of Nature (previous verse).

'*Wisdom is veiled by ignorance.*' Delusion about the Lord's involvement in action veils Nature's role in desire and action

(2.51) and experience (previous verse). Rid yourself of the notion of Divine intervention, reward and retribution!

Create Oneness:

5.16. *But for those whose ignorance is destroyed by Divine knowledge, Brahman is revealed as the Sun illuminates everything when it rises.*

Seeing Brahman's Oneness in all (4.18), we feel familiar with all (4.31), we know all (4.33). In this revelation of seeing Oneness of Brahman permeating all, we realize the omnipresent transcendent separate from us. The notion dawns, 'The transcendent is, in fact, real.'

We see Oneness of Brahman in everything. As the sun rises and destroys the darkness of night, the omnipresent transcendent destroys the veil of ignorance overshadowing Brahman's nature permeating all. Seeing is believing, destroying doubts about the transcendental nature of life.

5.17. *Those whose intellect is rooted in That, their Selves fixed in That, whose basis is That, cleansed of impurities by knowledge, go to the end of rebirth.*

'*That*' transcendent reality of Brahman permeates all. Cleansed of impurities by knowledge (previous verse), we see '*That*' which is Brahman backlighting everything.

Via the Gunas of Nature, we create what we see (3.05). Ego creates 1) experiencer of That, 2) experiencing That and 3) That experienced (5.14, 7.04 – 7.12). Having eliminated impurities from the nervous system through the practice of Karma Yoga (5.11), we actually "see" That backlighting all. Having created That, the intellect is rooted in That, the Self is fixed in That and our entire basis is That. And yet, seeing That confirms separation from That. We join eternal Brahman and *'go to the end of rebirth.'*

Achieve even vision:

5.18. *The enlightened see That in a cultivated and wise Brahmana, in a cow, in a dog, in an elephant and even one who has lost their cast.*

'The enlightened' have joined Brahman (previous verse).

The previous verse defines *'That'* unbounded and transcendent Golden Glue holding all in Oneness of Brahman.

Regardless of how the three Gunas manifest in outward appearances and inner qualities, the enlightened see *'That'* evenness among all beings: in the high cast of a Brahmana steeped in Vedic text; in a cow; in a dog; in an elephant; and even in one who has lost the path of evolution. *'The enlightened see That'* evenness in everything, in all action.

5.19. *Even here on earth, life is mastered by those whose mind is established in equanimity of Self. Evenness of Brahman is present in everything. Therefore, they are established in Brahman.*

'Life is mastered' by the nonactive and contented higher Self separate from the Gunas acting on the Gunas (3.28). Out of Self separate from action and the ego of lower self in union with Self, we create all action through the trinity of experience (3.05, 5.14, 5.17). Actions out of the Gunas of Nature and ego identified with Self naturally follow the course of evolution to the *'highest happiness'* (5.02). Mastery of life indeed.

When *'the mind is established in equanimity of Self,'* vision of lower self unites with equanimity of higher Self. Out of equanimity, we see evenness pervade all action. *'Evenness of Brahman is present in everything.'* We *'are established in Brahman.'*

5.20. *One who neither overly rejoices upon receiving what is pleasant nor grieves upon receiving what is unpleasant, whose intellect is steady, whose mind is undeluded, knowing Brahman, is established in Brahman.*

Reactions of joy and sorrow moderate in equanimity of Self (previous verse) and seeing the evenness of *'That'* in everything (5.17). We see those circumstances that cause either pleasant or unpleasant feelings in the even light of That. Experiencing evenness in cause, moderates effects of joy and sorrow.

We see the evenness of That permeating everything (previous verse). Experiencing the evenness of That steadies intellect and mind. Feelings of fullness and familiarity born of steadiness leave little room for doubt and delusion about the Reality and Truth we see.

We know Brahman by intellectually understanding the infusion of Brahman's Oneness into all creation and by directly experiencing That oneness by seeing It (4.18, previous verse). Truly *'knowing Brahman'* through understanding and experience, we become *'established in Brahman.'*

5.21. *He whose self remains unmoved by external sensations knows happiness in the Self. His Self united with Brahman through the Yoga of action, he enjoys imperishable happiness.*

Established in Brahman, evenness permeates circumstances and emotions they engender (previous two verses), promoting feelings of '*equanimity*' (5.19) and evening out the experience of '*external sensations.*' Evenness connects the experiencer and all that experienced. That is, evenness connects the experiencer with '*external sensations*'; this evenness linking experiencer and experienced is happiness (5.14). '*He whose self remains unmoved by external sensations knows happiness in the Self.*'

His Self united with Brahman through the Yoga of action' means that we continue to sacrifice desire through the practice of Karma Yoga, even after establishment in Brahman (5.19 – 5.20). The process of experiencing connects us to sacrificial acts, bestowing happiness (previous paragraph). We continue joyous acts of sacrifice with Brahman to achieve cosmic purpose (4.18).

Brahman is eternal. Established in Brahman (5.19 – 5.20) and working *with* Brahman to achieve cosmic purpose, we are eternal. '*He enjoys imperishable happiness*' in working with Brahman.

Attenuate agitation:

5.22. *All pleasures born of contact are wombs of pain. They begin and end, Arjuna. The enlightened seek not contentment in them.*

This verse contrasts the previous, where established in Brahman the sensation of evenness experienced in the process of experiencing renders happiness. In this verse, pleasures are born of contact rather than evenness linking experiencer and experienced. '*They* [contacts] *begin and end,*' as does the fleeting happiness they engender. '*The enlightened'* — those established in Brahman (5.19 – 5.20) — experience the even contentment of eternal happiness; pleasures born of contact pale in comparison. *'The enlightened seek not contentment in them.'*

5.23. *He who, even before liberation from the body, resist the agitation of desire and anger is disciplined. He is a happy man.*

The combined force of *'desire and anger'* is not a trifling matter and has earned the reputation of *'evil'* and *'enemy here on earth'*: *The force is desire; the force is anger. The force is born of Rajo Guna, all-consuming and most evil. Know this to be the enemy here on earth* (3.37).

The previous verse defines perfect discipline as the profound experience of eternal happiness. Therefore, seeing That evenness in everything (5.17), established in happiness (5.21) and unmoved by external sensations (previous verse) naturally attenuates *'desire and anger.'* Hence, we naturally *'resist the agitation'* born of desire and anger through our own happiness in contented Self.

See the transcendent:

5.24. *He who finds happiness from within, contentment from within and lit from within, this Yogi who finds eternal freedom in Brahman, attains Brahman Consciousness.*

'He who finds happiness from within' refers to verses 5.21 and 5.23: *'he enjoys eternal happiness'* and *'he is a happy man,'* respectively. Happiness does not come from external sources (5.22). Instead, he *'finds happiness from within'* in the process of "experiencing" born of Nature (5.14).

The enlightened seek not contentment in them [external contacts]' (5.22). Instead, the enlightened naturally turn within. *'Established in Brahman'* (5.19 – 5.20), the sensation of evenness comes from within, rendering equanimity, inner contentment and happiness.

Via Nature and refined qualities of ego, we create That light [of Brahman] from within we see illuminating all (5.16 – 5.17).

Though Brahman causes all action, Brahman remains uninvolved in action (4.18). Consequently, Brahman is the highwater mark of renunciation from action. Established in Brahman (5.19 – 5.20), we too live in *'eternal freedom'* of action born of our renunciation of action. We silently witness our actions go of Nature's accord to further spiritual and material evolution, seeing the light of That, content and happy from within, *'This Yogi who finds eternal freedom in Brahman* [from within], *attains Brahman Consciousness,'* attains eternal renunciation.

Continued in next verse.

5.25. *The seers, sins destroyed and doubts dispelled, whose selves are controlled, who delights in the welfare of all beings, attains the freedom of Brahman.*

'Seers' see the Self as separate from activity, silently witness life go of Nature's accord to further spiritual and material evolution, see Oneness of Brahman in everything, "experience" evenness in all, and finally, actually see the transcendent.

'Sins [are] *destroyed'* only when one does not act in any way whatsoever. Established in the renunciation of Brahman (previous verse), sinful acts are impossible. In addition, establishment in the nonaction of Brahman shields us from the

consequences of past actions. [4.36; 5.10: *'Acting in accord with Brahman, having abandoned attachments, his acts are untainted by sin as a lotus leaf by water.'*]

'Doubts dispelled.' Feelings of fullness born from experiencing evenness, happiness and steady intellect, and seeing the transcendent, dispel doubt about the separation of Self from the relative. That is, dispel doubts about renunciation from action.

'Whose selves are controlled' by the *'Self of all beings'* (5.07). The lower self is individuality. In Cosmic Consciousness the lower self unites with higher Self; individual unites with universal. Oneness of Brahman is universal on all levels of experience. Seeing Oneness of Brahman in all beings, including ourselves, the lower self gains universality in the Oneness of That. In this way, liberation in universality of Self controls individuality of self by permeating self with That (5.17 – 5.18; also for "control," see verse 2.61).

'Who delights in the welfare of all beings.' We see That Oneness of Brahman in ourselves and all beings (5.18). Out of universal Oneness, identification with all beings, evenness (5.18 – 5.19), and happiness (5.21 – 5.24). We delight in the welfare of all beings we create through ego for the purpose of happiness.

'Attains the freedom of Brahman.' Being the eternal non-doer, Brahman renounces action. Established in Brahman (5.19 – 5.20), we achieve freedom in renunciation from action (previous verse). In addition, delighting in the welfare of all beings renders feelings of kinship with all, which in turn, lift us above the confines of isolation and selfish individuality. Separate from all by seeing That in all beings (5.17), we feel liberated from selfish feelings, thoughts and actions in our love of all.

5.26. *For disciplined men who have cast away desire and anger, whose thoughts are controlled, who know the Self, freedom of Brahman exists in everything.*

Disciplined men established in Brahman (5.19 – 5.20), acting to fulfill cosmic purpose, renounce action (5.24 – 5.25). Rising to the bait of strong emotions naturally lies outside the experience of '*disciplined men*' (5.23).

Living in the Self separate from action and unmoved by external sensations, they cast off desire and anger (5.23). Individuality of lower self '*mastered*' by realizing the universality of higher Self, '*thoughts are controlled*' by evenness of steady intellect (5.07, 5.19, previous verse). Being established in Brahman, '*freedom of Brahman* [that is, renunciation from action] *exists in everything* because Brahman is in all things (4.18).

Attain peace:

5.27. *Leaving external contacts outside, attention settles within the eyebrows, even inhalation and exhalation moves through the nostrils*

In previous verses we go to the end of rebirth (5.17), know Brahman (5.20), become established in Brahman (5.19 – 5.20), unite with Brahman (5.21) and attain Brahman Consciousness (5.24).

Having renounced all actions (previous verse), we leave '*external contacts outside.*' We abandon effects external contacts have on the flow of consciousness. Happy and content within, awareness settles into the spiritual center '*within the eyebrows.*' Breathing — exchange of inner and outer; experiencing linking experiencer and experienced (5.13

– 5.14) — steadies to an even stream of consciousness. This evenness of *'inhalation and exhalation moving through the nostrils'* fills the senses, mind, intellect, and the universe.

5.28. *The sage whose senses, mind and intellect are controlled, from whom desires, fear and anger have departed, is forever liberated.*

The experience of all-pervading evenness (previous verse) *'controls* [evens functioning of] *senses, mind and intellect.'* Abandoning *'external contacts'* (previous verse), the evils of *'desires, fear, and anger'* engendered by them depart. Feelings of happiness well-up from within, liberating us from attachments and bondage to action. Consequently, we are *'forever liberated'* from action; we have renounced all action forever; we live in the present amidst Nature's administration of desire and action.

5.29. *Having known Me, the enjoyer of sacrifices and austerities, The Mighty Lord of all the world and friend to all beings, he attains peace.*

"So God created man in His own image, in the image of God He created him." — *Genesis* 1:27.

'Me,' that is, Lord Krishna is the enjoyer of *'sacrifices'* (4.24 – 4.30) and *'austerities'* (4.10 – 4.14); *'Mighty Lord of all the world'* who informs Nature to carry out His creation (4.05 – 4.06, 5.14); and supporter of happiness and *'friend to all beings'* (5.25).

"Form follows function," Louis Sullivan. Forever liberated from attachment and bondage to action — that is, living in the present (previous verse) — we naturally function from His level of consciousness. We inherently 'sacrifice' desire to support life and evolution (5.10 – 5.11). Purified through action to achieve cosmic purpose of universal happiness, we enjoy the 'austerities' of higher Self separate from indulgent lower self (5.07, 5.11). Through Nature via the ego, we create our 'world' and the happiness governing its functioning (5.14 – 5.21). Befriending all by bestowing expansion of happiness into creation, we delight in the welfare of 'all beings' (5.25). Immersed in the even happiness of our creation, we operate above agitation of desire and anger (5.23). Having 'cast away' strong emotions, 'thoughts controlled' by the all-pervasive evenness flooding the universe (previous verse), knowing the 'Self' as renounced from action, and forever experiencing the 'freedom of Brahman' in all creation (5.26), calmness separates Self from action. We attain 'peace' in Brahman Consciousness. Dharma wanes (Ch 6).

Appendix 2: God Consciousness — See God Everywhere

Overview of Ch 6:

Practice Union. Feel happiness abiding in the heart unite Self with action. Achieve even vision. See God everywhere.

Calmness trumps action: 1 Sanyasi and Yogi perform actions to achieve Brahman Consciousness. 2 Both paths renounce fruits of action and relinquish incentive of desire. 3 As achieving Brahman Consciousness required action, achieving God Consciousness requires calmness. 4 In Brahman Consciousness, calmness separates Self from action.

Higher Self befriends lower self: 5&6 Higher Self calms lower self. On the other hand, having failed to calm lower self, self disrupts Self. 7 Having been conquered, the self remains steadfast in dualities of physical, emotional and psychological provocations. 8 Such a Yogi has conquered the senses and remains unshakable. 9 This Yogi is equal minded, neutral, impartial, and rises above the fray on the merit of calmness alone.

Self returns to Self: 10 Having conquered the lower self with calmness of higher Self, calmness is the means by which Self returns to Self (Self-referral) when distracted by self. In this way, Self spontaneously maintains calmness of Self, which in turn calms lower self.

Liberation: Self-referral affects body, mind and spirit by 11 promoting positive spiritual energy, 12 purifying lower self, 13 steadying awareness, 14 opening the mind to Transcendent Self, and 15 achieving supreme liberation in the Transcendent.

Moderation: 16&17 Moderate actions advance Self-referral and maintain liberation.

Yoga (Union): Having achieved Brahman Consciousness, practice Yoga. Directly practice Union by Union itself. 18 Absorbed in the calm nature of Self, free yourself from cravings. 19 Subdue thoughts opposed to spiritual evolution. 20&21 Content in Self beheld by the Self, achieve lasting happiness. 22 There is no higher gain than lasting happiness. 23 Practice this Yoga (Union sustaining Union) without doubt and an undismayed mind.

Self-referral: 24 Self-referral is the practice of Union. Self-referral befriends the wandering mind back to the calming influence of higher Self. 25 Nature informs intellect established in Self to return to calm Self. 26 On becoming aware of the mind wavering to and fro, Self refers back to Self, sheltering lower self under its umbrella of calmness. 27 Become one with Brahman and achieve supreme happiness. 28 Contact Brahman and achieve lasting happiness.

God Consciousness: 29 See the Self in all beings and all beings in the Self. 30 See God everywhere. 31 Dwell in God. 32 See all in evenness of God Consciousness.

Discipline and maintenance: 33&34 How can we see evenness when the mind has a mind of its own and by nature is unstable, turbulent, powerful, and downright obstinate? 35&36 True enough, the mind has a mind of its own but by practicing Self-referral, the mind is held in lasting happiness abiding in the heart. Yoga (Union) is not for the lazy, dull, indulgent, or indifferent. Keep your eye on the ball.

Path taken: 37 - 39 What happens to the aspirant who falls from the path? 40 There is never destruction for someone who performs right actions. 41&42 The aspirant is reborn into pure and illustrious circumstances or better yet, into a family of Yogis. 43&44 One regains knowledge and continues along the path. 45 Through perseverance and many births the

transcendent goal is reached. 46 Be a Yogi. Act. 47 Perform
right actions. Practice Karma Yoga. Merge with God.

Commentary on Ch 6 verses 1 – 47:

Calmness trumps action:

6.01. *He who performs their duty, while renouncing fruits of action, is a Sanyasi and a Yogi; not he who lights no fire and fails to perform actions.*

Actions to further evolution differ for '*Sanyasi*' and '*Yogi,*' the act of contemplation for the Sanyasi, and mental and physical actions to achieve outcomes for the '*Yogi.*' The Sanyasi achieves contentment and happiness by revelation of Self separate from action (3.05). The Yogi achieves contentment and happiness by direct experience of Self separate from action (3.05). Inner states of contentment and happiness naturally eliminate desire for fruits and the actions desires seed to attain fruits. Actions and fruits are completely renounced on the level of Brahman. For both Sanyasi and Yogi, paths of action have achieved their purpose. Sanyasi and Yogi experience peace in Brahman Consciousness (5.29).

He without desire and energy to achieve higher states of consciousness ('*no fire*') and he '*who … fails to perform actions*' to further spiritual evolution will neither perform '*their duty*' nor renounce '*fruits of action.*' Such a man lives on the horizontal plane of life. For him, ephemeral states of happiness and contentment compose a life of attachment and bondage, a life in ignorance of Self separate from action. He finds no '*peace*' in Brahman Consciousness (5.29).

6.02. *Know that called Sanyasi to be Yoga. No one becomes a Yogi without relinquishing the incentive of desire.*

The previous verse drew on the elimination of desire for fruits and renunciation of action to show equal footing for accomplished Sanyasi and Yogi. This verse drills deeper into the *'incentive of desire.'*

'No one becomes a Yogi without relinquishing the incentive of desire.' The Yogi, experiencing the fullness of union with Brahman relinquishes incentive of desire (4.19). In union with Brahman, he sees evenness (5.19 - 5.21), erasing distinctions between this and that. Seeing Brahman's creation of good and increase in everything (4.18), everything promises happiness equally. Fruits lose their unique appeal to promise happiness. For the Yogi, incentive is gone.

Krishna points out the same is true for the Sanyasi, in union with Brahman the Sanyasi too has lost *'the incentive of desire.'*

Krishna's take-home message: accomplished Sanyasi and Yogi attain peace with separation of Self from activity in Brahman consciousness. In peace desire and incentive evaporate in renunciation of action. Paths of Sanyasi and Yogi have merged. Both have achieved complete renunciation of action in the *'peace'* of Brahman consciousness. Action has run its course. Dharma wanes (next verse).

6.03. *For the aspirant wishing to ascend to Yoga, action is said to be the means; for one who has ascended to Yoga, calmness is said to be the means.*

This verse lies central to this chapter and gaining God Consciousness.

Brahman Consciousness stands atop Mt Yoga. *'Duty'* (6.01) accomplished the ascent. We stand as Brahman, free from desire, action and even incentive of desire (6.02).

'For one who has ascended to Yoga, calmness is said to be the means.' *'Calmness'* maintains Self separate from action. Deep within, calmness of Self defines us at all times. Calmness of its own accord — no action required — furthers

evolution. Indeed, 'Calmness [and only calmness] *is said to be the means.'*

Many authors hold '*Calmness is said to be the means*' as the practice of meditation to achieve calmness. They appear to forget that meditation is action and that calmness separating Self from actions has been achieved in Brahman Consciousness. Fact is, '*calmness*' — and only '*calmness*' — is the means to attaining God Consciousness (6.10; 6.24 - 6.28).

6.04. *One who has ascended to Yoga is neither attached to objects of the senses nor to actions to experience them. He has relinquished all incentive of desire.*

Having ascended Mt Yoga, the Self stands calm and Self-sufficient and needs nothing. Calmness precludes the draw of happiness promised in objects of the senses and consequently, attachments to those objects and selfish desire and action to experience them. Self-sufficient calmness vanquishes the incentive of desire to find happiness in disruptive objects of the senses.

Higher Self befriends lower self:

6.05. *Let a man raise his self by his Self. Let him not degrade his Self. For the Self alone can be a friend to the self. Or the Self alone can be an enemy to the self.*

Higher Self influences lower self and *vice-versa*. Calmness of higher Self '*raises the self by the Self.*' We feel, think and act calmly under the influence of Self's calmness. On the other hand, '*Let him not degrade his Self*' by letting lower self agitate higher Self and overshadow the experience of calmness. Choose calmness; do not run away with agitated self; let not the self '*degrade*' calmness of Self.

Higher Self is lower self's only friend and a good one: possessed of calmness, reliable and willing to help. 'For the Self alone can be a friend to the self' by rendering calmness to it. 'Or the Self alone can be an enemy to the self.' When higher Self's calmness is lost to lower self's agitation, lower self suffers without relief from higher Self.

6.06. *For him who has conquered the self by the Self, the Self is a friend. But for him who has not conquered the self by the Self, the Self remains hostile like an enemy.*

In Brahman Consciousness, higher Self conquers lower self by infusing it with calmness. In this case *'the Self is a friend'* (previous verse). *'But for him who has not conquered the self by the Self,'* lower self agitates higher Self and the calming influence of Self is lost. It is as if higher Self has turned its back on the lower self and lets it stew in sticky juices of bondage. *'The Self remains hostile like an enemy'* because it fails to share its calmness. Indeed, blame lies squarely on higher Self for letting lower self get away with it.

6.07. *For him who conquers the self, who remains deep in peace, the Self remains steadfast in cold, heat, pleasure, and pain. Too, in honor and disgrace.*

'Deep in peace' of Brahman Consciousness (5.29), *'calmness'* of Self pervades the mind of lower self (previous verse), steadying it in extreme dualities of *'cold, heat … honor and disgrace.'* Extremes dualities in physical, emotional and psychological stimuli fail to overshadow the influence of calmness higher Self has on lower self, mutually benefiting the Self and self, and forever leaving Self *'steadfast'* in peace of Brahman Consciousness (5.29).

6.08. *The Yogi is united who is contented in knowledge and experience, who is unshakable with conquered senses, who earth, stone and gold are the same. He attains enlightenment.*

Here, '*knowledge*' is a matter of understanding the underlying nature of calmness to befriend the self (6.05 - 6.06). Feeling calm in the helter-skelter of daily life conjures an undeniable experience of Self calming self. Thinking and feeling unite in conquering the senses. Calmness maintains equal and indifferent sensation of '*earth, stone and gold*' regardless of touch, usefulness and value. We experience Oneness of Brahman through all the senses.

6.09. *He who is equal-minded toward friends, companions, and enemies, who is neutral among enemies and kinsmen, and who is impartial among righteous and evil-doers, is distinguished among men.*

Here, Krishna addresses the nature of silent calmness, every ready to address situations from a wellspring of full potential unencumbered by preconception and judgment.

'*Equal-minded,*' naturally he lives in the silence of calmness and considers all in the same light regardless of expectations of harmony and disharmony. '*Neutral among enemies and kinsmen*' inherently he remains balanced in silent calmness, equally ready to address aggression and acceptance appropriately. '*Impartial among righteous and evil-doers,*' he instinctively remains unbiased, confident and fearless in the silence of calmness regardless of perceived effect on evolution.

'*Distinguished,*' an equal-minded, neutral and impartial person rises above the fray on the merit of inner and outer calmness.

Self returns to Self:

6.10. *The Yogi always collects himself on the Self; remaining in seclusion, alone, his mind and body calmed, desiring nothing and free of possessions.*

'*The Yogi* [having gained Brahman Consciousness] *always collects himself on the Self*' by referring the Self to the Self. '*Calmness is said to be the means*' of the calm Self moving the lower self back to the calm nature of Self. In union Self and self act as one. When the self takes attention away from inner calmness of Self to some agitated state, the Self naturally comes home to Self and moves lower self back to calmness, '*his mind and body calmed.*' (6.05 - 6.07).

On its own, the calm Self '*always*' chooses to remain in the calm '*seclusion*' of Self. [This is Nature's hand at play, verses 6.24 – 6.28, 6.35 – 6.36.] '*Alone*' refers to the complete separation of Self from action in the unifying '*peace*' of Brahman Consciousness (5.29). Unmoving and nonactive Self refers attention to silent and unmoving Self when pulled away from it by wavering lower self, gently returning the mind's attention to calmness, reclaiming the wavering mind of lower self to the calm nature of Self in one with it.

Self-referral comes naturally to those who have ascended Mt Yoga and attained Brahman Consciousness (by '*action is said to be the means*, 6.03). They have achieved calmness which maintains Self separate from action. Established in calmness of Self, Self unerringly brings Self back to Self ('*calmness is said to be the means*' 6.03), truly '*no effort is forfeited and no obstacle to completion exists*' (2.40).

To force calmness and Self-referral merely makes a mood of them, mocking Self-awareness and retarding evolution.

Liberation:

The following five verses document the gross to subtle effects of Self returning to Self (previous verse) on neurophysiology, attention, Self-awareness, submission, and liberation.

6.11. *Finding a firm seat for himself in a clean place, neither too high nor too low, covered with kusha grass, deerskin and cloth,*

Neurophysiology: The natural impulse to return back to calm Self (previous verse) in a settled state conducive to Union (*'seated'*), spontaneously cleanses the mind of negative thoughts (*'clean place'*), frees the mind from dualities (*'neither too high nor too low'*), and insulates from negative energy (*'kusha grass'*), while promoting comfort and the upward flow of positive spiritual energy (*'deerskin and cloth'*).

6.12. *Seated there, the mind one-pointed, activity of mind and senses subdued, practicing Yoga* [Union of Self referring to Self] *for self-purification.*

Attention: Self-sufficient and separate from action (*'seated there'*), Self referring to Self (*'the mind one pointed'*), *'mind and senses* [of lower self] *subdued'* by calmness of Self, Self-referral (6.10, 6.24 – 6.28; *'practicing Union'*), Self befriends and purifies self with its silent calmness (*'self-purification'*).

6.13. *The body, head and neck upright and still, his gaze directed to the front of his nose, and not looking in any direction,*

Self-awareness: Spiritual energy flowing upward without obstacles (*'the body, head and neck upright and still'*), Self-directed attention looking forward to the limits of self without expectation (*'his gaze directed to the front of his nose'*), awareness naturally steadied on the Self by the Self (*'not looking in any direction'*).

6.14. *With quieted mind, casting out fear, established in the vow of chastity, the mind and thoughts fixed on Me, sitting realizing Me as the Transcendent.*

Submission: Mind calmed (*'with quieted mind* [of self]' befriended by higher Self; 6.05), contented and balanced (*'casting out fear'*), Self-sufficient (*'established in the vow of chastity'*), attention on the transcendent Self (*'thoughts fixed on Me, sitting realizing Me as the Transcendent'*).

6.15. *Thus, continually disciplining himself, the Yogi whose mind is subdued goes to peace, goes to the supreme liberation abiding in Me.*

Liberation: Self-referral calming wavering lower self (*'continually disciplining himself* in the practice of Self-referral, verses 6.10; 6.24 – 6.28), *the Yogi whose mind is subdued'* in the *'peace'* of Brahman Consciousness (*'goes to peace'*), and calmness upholding separation of Self from action (*'goes to the supreme liberation* [from action] *abiding in Me'*).

Moderation:

6.16. *Yoga is not for him who eats too much or eats nothing at all. It is not for him who sleeps too much or for him who keeps awake.*

This verse and the following verse address the importance of moderate behavior to maintain balance in body and mind necessary for sustaining Self-referral and achieving liberation (previous five verses).

Excess in eating (or fasting) and excess in sleeping (or maintaining wakefulness) dull the mind and the spontaneity of Self-referral. Excessive behavior of self puts a strain on higher Self's faculty to befriend and reign it in with calmness (6.05).

6.17. *For him moderate in food and recreation, moderate in all actions, and moderate in sleeping and waking, Yoga destroys all sorrows.*

Avoid excesses in daily life which unbalance the body and mind, undermining the Self and self acting as one. Moderation maintains a nervous system capable of supporting the natural balance of Self-referral (6.10; 6.24 – 6.28). In moderation, the self remains within the range of Self's friendship and calming influence.

We respond to loss with sorrow. Krishna uses '*sorrows*' here to underscore the loss of friendship between Self and self. Even with a painful loss in friendship, Self-referral kicks in, reestablishing the friendship and furthering evolution to God consciousness, given we remain moderate in actions.

Yoga (Union):

6.18. *When his mind is absorbed in the Self, established, and when he is free from craving pleasure, then he is said to be united.*

'*Absorbed in the Self*,' the mind of lower self settles into calmness of Self (6.10; 6.24 – 6.28). '*Alone*' indicates that the mind has abandoned the field of activity altogether and does not associate with objects. The mind becomes '*established*' in the calmness of Self. Mind in union with fulfilling calmness of Self (6.05) overrides the need to crave pleasures.

6.19. *As a lamp in a windless place does not flicker, to such compare the Yogi of subdued thought practicing Yoga with the Self.*

Practicing '*Yoga with Self*' means Self-referral (6.10; 6.24 – 6.28).

With the mind having abandoned the field of activity altogether and established in Self's calmness (previous verse), an overriding feeling of tranquility subdues the need for thoughts extraneous to furthering evolution, '*as a lamp in a windless place does not flicker*.'

6.20. *When thought comes to rest, settled through the practice of Yoga, beholding the Self by the Self alone, he is content in the Self.*

In the verse 6.18 the mind was absorbed in the Self alone. Here the Self beholds '*the Self by the Self alone.*'

'*When thought comes to rest*' deepens the experience of '*subdued thought*' (previous verse). Self-referral is '*the practice of Yoga,*' where the calm Self remains in the calm seclusion of Self alone (6.10; 6.24 – 6.28): '*beholding the Self by the Self alone.*' '*Alone*' underscores the Self-sufficiency of Self-referral. Self-sufficient, '*he is content in the Self.*'

6.21. *He knows lasting happiness, lying beyond the senses and grasped by the intellect, and established there, does not deviate from the truth.*

The senses experience limited happiness in the objective world. '*Lasting happiness*' lies beyond the senses in the transcendent. The intellect discerns what is real and true. When the ego, the subtlest quality of intellect (2.39), identifies with Self perpetually beholding the Self (previous verse), it grasps the '*lasting happiness*' of Self. Having grasped the lasting happiness of this Truth realized by the ego, 'I am lasting happiness,' the intellect surrenders to this Truth and does not deviate from it.

6.22. *Having gained this, he cannot imagine any other gain as higher. Established in this, he is unmoved, even by profound sorrow.*

'*Having gained* [the truth of] *this*' lasting happiness and remaining aligned with it (previous verse), '*he cannot imagine any other gain as higher.*' Krishna declares that happiness is top drawer. We have reached an endpoint, or in fact, a turning point, as we shall see in verse 6.32.

Previously 'Yoga destroys all sorrow' (6.17) under moderate actions and calmness of higher Self's friendship with lower self (6.05). Hence, sorrow was an entity to be delt with through calmness. 'Lasting happiness' supersedes calmness (see also verse 6.32). 'Established in this [lasting happiness], he is unmoved, even by profound sorrow.' That is, even with the loss of friendship with lower self, the higher Self remains Self-sufficient.

6.23. *Let this disconnection with sorrow be known as Yoga; this Yoga is to be practiced without doubt and an undismayed mind.*

'Let this disconnection with sorrow be known as Yoga [Union].' When the intellect unites, achieves Yoga and grasps 'lasting happiness' (previous two verses), Self completely disconnects from sorrow.

The following five verses illustrate how 'this Yoga [Union] is to be practiced without doubt and an undismayed mind.'

Self-referral:

Brahman Consciousness required.

6.24. *Abandoning those desires whose origins lie in one's incentives, controlling the multitude of senses with the mind.*

Self-referral is the spontaneous practice of Union: Self referring to Self and through its calmness, befriending self (6.10). The surface of the mind wavers with 'those desires whose origins lie in one's incentives.' Separated from desire and action in Brahman Consciousness, Nature activates Self-referral. In becoming aware of the drift away from calmness on the surface of the mind, Nature's purpose to further evolution kicks Self-referral into gear, returning Self and self to calmness of Self. 'No effort is forfeited and no obstacle to completion exists' (2.40) in 'controlling the multitude of senses *with the mind'* by *'this Yoga [which] is to be practiced without doubt and an undismayed mind'* (6.23).

6.25. Gradually he should come to rest through the intellect firmly grasped; his mind established in the Self, he should not think of anything.

This verse drills down into the process revealed in the previous verse.

'Gradually he should come to rest through the intellect firmly grasped.' The intellect decides the real and true course of action to further evolution. Nature informs refined qualities of intellect established in Self to return to calmness of Self (previous verse). His mind thus befriended by Self (6.05), *'he should not think of anything'* and just let go to Self-referral (previous verse).

6.26. Whenever the fickle mind, wavers to and fro, let him bring it back under the sway of the Self alone.

'Him' is the dweller in the body (3.40), the individualized nature of the Self.

On becoming aware of thoughts witnessed on the surface of the mind wavering to and fro, go with the flow. Let Nature shift attention back to calmness of Self: *'let him bring it back under the sway of the Self alone'* (6.24). *'Let'* underscores leaving desire and action to Nature to disengage the mind from wavering to and fro, seemingly returning Self to calmness of Self of its own accord.

6.27. The Yogi whose mind is peaceful, in whom incentives are calmed, whose mind is free from evil, and has become one with Brahman, attains supreme happiness.

The '*mind is peaceful*' by letting go of thoughts on its surface level (previous verse) and letting calmness of Self befriend self (6.05), where incentives are calmed by referral of Self back to Self and infusing self with calmness (6.24). Nature decides which thoughts support evolution and are worthy of pursuit, or not. Thus, we free ourselves from evil thoughts that retard evolution by spontaneously turning control back to Nature and allowing calmness of Self to befriend self (6.05).

In the supreme peace of Brahman Consciousness, we attain '*supreme happiness.*' Having attained Brahman Consciousness (5.24) and supreme peace of mind in separation from activity (5.29), we achieve '*supreme happiness.*' From verse 2.66, '*For one lacking peace of mind, can there be happiness*?

6.28. *Practicing this Yoga, the Yogi, freed from evil actions, easily attains contact with Brahman and attains lasting happiness.*

Freed from evil thoughts (previous verse), freed from '*evil actions*' evil thoughts engender. In Brahman Consciousness (5.24) we easily contact Brahman. That is, we attain Brahman's complete separation from action. In perpetual Self-referral and fueled by Nature's never-ending purpose to direct desires and actions towards furthering evolution (6.24), '*supreme happiness*' in Brahman Consciousness (previous verse) lasts.

God Consciousness:

6.29. *Established in Yoga, with even vision he sees the Self in all beings and sees all beings present in the Self.*

Seeing the Self in all beings and all beings in the Self, we simultaneously see transcendent and relative. Transcendent Brahman resides in everything relative (4.18). With '*even vision*' gained in contact with Brahman (previous verse) we see transcendent Oneness of Brahman in all the relative beings we see (4.18). That is, seeing Oneness of Brahman in all beings, we simultaneously see transcendent and relative.

Or considered in a brighter light, the Self of all beings is the individual manifesting out of the unbounded field of pure consciousness. Just before this first manifestation of consciousness forms individual ego, this Self-same consciousness pervades all beings. We are all one. In even vision, we see this familiar evenness in all beings. It's as plain as the nose on your face: I am that; thou art that. And therefore human 'beings' standout against the backdrop of creation. We recognize our Selves in others.

6.30. *He who sees Me everywhere and sees all things in Me, I am not lost to him and He is not lost to Me.*

This verse amps up seeing the Self in all beings to seeing Me everywhere.

In '*even vision*' (previous verse) we see the transcendent made manifest everywhere. The feeling of spiritual unity prevails. Out of spiritual unity in feeling, thinking and acting, we experience God on the sensory level and '*He is not lost to me.*'

Or considered in a brighter light, the essence of the Creator lies in all creation (3.15). With the marvel of '*even vision*' we see that essence which underlies seeing Oneness of Brahman in everything, everywhere.

6.31. *Established in Union with Me, he who honors Me abiding in all beings, in whatever way he acts, that Yogi abides in Me.*

'*Established in Union with me,*' amps up not being lost to Me (previous verse) to abiding in Me.

In his commentary on this verse Maharishi Mahesh Yogi uses the perfect analogy: when wearing golden spectacles, we see gold everywhere. *'Established in Union with Me,'* we see God everywhere (previous verse).

Seeing everything with *'even vision'* stimulates us to act accordingly, *'that Yogi abides in Me.'* Abiding in Me brings *'honors'* down to earth. *'In all beings'* is where we see God, not as a hypothetical, bearded, stern, and robed character enthroned on puffy clouds. You need only open your eyes. Wearing golden spectacles, you see *'Me everywhere'* (previous verse). The following verse continues this *'even vision.'*

6.32. *Seeing everything with an even vision in the image of the Self, Arjuna, be it pleasure or pain, he is thought to be the Supreme Yogi.*

This verse amps up the previous from considerations of *'Me'* to the intensity of seeing everything through the transcendent Self.

Unifying *'lasting happiness'* (6.28) abiding in the heart outshines *'calmness'* and brings senses, feelings, thinking, and vision in tune with it. Through the lens of Self in the *'lasting happiness'* of Self, we see evenness of God's love everywhere. Separation of Self from action dissolves. This is knowledge. We visually experience God's love everywhere. We feel familiar with that experience. Through familiarity, we know the Truth: All is love; Love is all. On the level of feeling, it just makes sense.

The lens of Self sees evenness everywhere. Distinctions between dualities, including extreme dualities of *'pleasure or pain,'* fail to arise in the Supreme Yogi's even vison. We sense differences and respond to them appropriately but the experiences themselves have no sticking power and leave no impression to influence future actions (2.39).

"God met me more than halfway. He freed me from my anxious fears." — *Psalm* 34:4. God Consciousness is active, not passive. In fact, it is participatory. Through sharing '*even vision*,' we achieve God Consciousness. Out of ego, we create the "experience" of '*even vision*' that Vishnu the Sustainer sustains [as in 5.14 (experiencing happiness), 5.17 (experiencing That Oneness pervading all), 5.19 - 5.21 (experiencing evenness)]. '*That Yogi abides in* Me [Krishna, Vishnu incarnate]' who partners with Me in creating '*even vision*.' I sustain '*That Yogi*.'

Brahman seen in '*evenness*' in all things (5.19 - 5.24) differs from '*even vision*' of seeing God everywhere (this verse). We see evenness of Brahman in objects. We see '*even vision*' of God in '*the image of the Self*.' '*Evenness*' in all things is observational; '*even vision*' everywhere is participatory. Where we once saw Oneness in everything, we now see God everywhere. We see joy everywhere. We see joy in all creation.

Seeing joy in all creation deepens knowledge. Previously we defined knowledge as seeing Oneness in all, becoming familiar with all and consequently, knowing all (4.33). Seeing joy in all creation, gives purpose to the Oneness we see. Self-referral — '*calmness is said to be the means*' (6.03) — has purified the nervous systems to the degree where we experience creation manifesting out of all possibilities. [In consensus Physics, the wave function collapses out of all possibilities, the Veda.] Knowing God at the action level of His purpose, so to speak, we call God Consciousness. This is the beginning of pure knowledge. Subsequent chapters deepen understanding and experience beyond God's purpose and reveal deeper meaning to action and to fundamentals of knowledge. So, even as we round the bend in Ch 6, we have yet to reach the nub of knowledge.

Mathew 5:5 ("Blessed are the meek; for they shall inherit the earth.") helps to summarize levels of consciousness addressed so far and their evolving states of knowledge.

In Transcendental Consciousness, "Liberated are those who sacrifice desire by serving others' desires; for they shall feel at home in the world they were born into"; know freedom from action.

In Cosmic Consciousness, "Contented are those who spontaneously perform right actions; for they shall feel at home in the world they were born into"; know desires and actions go of their own accord.

In Brahman Consciousness, "Peaceful are those who experience calmness separating higher Self from lower self; for they shall feel at home in the world they were born into"; know happiness in all creation.

In God Consciousness, "Joyful are those who see God everywhere; for they shall feel at home in the world they were born into"; know God at the action level of His purpose.

Truly, consciousness structures knowledge (Rik Veda). Also see Appendix 4: States of Consciousness in a Nutshell.

Continued in 6.35.

Discipline and maintenance:

From verse 3.39, '*This insatiable flame of desire veils wisdom and is the eternal enemy of the wise.*'

6.33. Arjuna: *This Yoga declared by You as evenness of mind, O Krishna, because of wavering I do not see its continuance.*

If the nature of the fickle mind is to waver, as Krishna stated (6.26), how is it possible for '*evenness of mind*' to endure?

6.34. Arjuna continues: *For the mind, indeed, is unstable, turbulent, powerful, and obstinate; I consider it as difficult to control as the wind.*

How so *'evenness of mind'* (6.32) when the mind drags Arjuna here and there beyond his fixity of purpose?

6.35. Krishna: *Without doubt, the mind is wavering and difficult to control, Arjuna, but by practice of nonattachment, it is held.*

Evolution supports innovative minds that think outside the box and *vice-versa*. Krishna agrees, *'the* [surface level of the] *mind is wavering and difficult to control.'* For such is the mind's independent nature in strategizing survival and increase in the entropy of daily life. Indeed, *'wavering and difficult to control'* is a fact of the mind's independent functioning in the relative field. It's a good thing.

The entropic universe we live in easily disrupts the thin vision of joy we create in our tripartite experience (3.05). *'But by practice of nonattachment, it* [the mind] *is held.'* By this Krishna means the practice of Union, spontaneous Self-referral to seeing God everywhere, to seeing joy everywhere. You do not have to drift off with wavering thoughts witnessed on the surface of mind. Having achieved Brahman Consciousness and complete separation of Self from action (5.29; 6.03), we are no longer obliged to feed the beast. *'Practice of nonattachment,'* naturally returning to seeing God everywhere, is necessary to sustain God Consciousness and joy.

By practice of nonattachment, the mind is *'held'* in *'lasting happiness'* of God Consciousness. Nature no longer decides on Self-referral (6.24); it does not have to. *'Held'* means sustained. Joy sustains joy; but it is a very delicate matter, fueled by gratitude and requiring Vishnu's participation as well. Sustained by Vishnu (aka Krishna, 6.32), happiness resides in the heart's influence on senses, feeling, thoughts, and evenness of vision. Even in the helter-skelter dynamics of everyday life, happiness cradles the busy mind in the warm glow of joy.

"God helps those [sustain '*lasting happiness*'] who help themselves" (following verse).

6.36. *I agree Yoga is difficult to attain for him who is undisciplined; but it can be gained through proper means by him who endeavors.*

"I think you should bear in mind that entropy is not on your side," Elon Musk. Loss of friendship between Self and self is entropic (6.05). Defeat entropy by living in the present. Gratitude exists only in the present. Simply be grateful for seeing God everywhere. Stop entropy. Feel increase.

Krishna acknowledges, '*Yoga*' (Union) in God Consciousness and seeing God everywhere requires discipline. But God Consciousness can be gained through the proper means of seeing God everywhere through the practice of nonattachment (previous verse). '*Endeavors*' means to practice '*Yoga*' (Union); practicing Union in partnership with Vishnu is not for the lazy, dull, indulgent, or indifferent. Meet Vishnu halfway or He'll drop you like a hot potato. Gaining and sustaining God Consciousness and seeing the universal fabric of joy everywhere requires discipline. Get with the program!

Path taken:

6.37. Arjuna asks: *One who is undisciplined, though possessed of faith, whose mind has fallen from Yoga and does not achieve perfection, what does he gain*?

Battle focuses the mind on killing and survival. Will Arjuna not stray from the path by taking attention off Krishna and the practice of nonattachment? What if he dies on the field of battle before liberation? Has he been disciplined and endeavored enough?

6.38. Arjuna continues: *Does he not perish like a broken cloud, without foothold and fallen from both worlds, deluded on the path of Brahman?*

Physically destroyed in the battle of life, is his spiritual progress also destroyed? '*Fallen from both worlds*' of heaven and earth, does he lose footing gained?

6.39. Arjuna continues: *You are able, Krishna, to completely dispel my doubts; none but you can dispel my uncertainty.*

Arjuna submits to pure knowledge.

Hope springs eternal. Krishna has dispelled doubts before. Such is the '*faith*' (6.37) Krishna has instilled in Arjuna.

6.40. Krishna responds: *Neither here on earth nor in heaven above is there destruction for him who acts uprightly. No one who does good goes the way of misfortune.*

Krishna immediately returns to the theme of practicing Karma Yoga and performing right action. With even a taste of liberation, Arjuna will realize its depth and continuity. Fight and he will not be destroyed like a broken cloud and go the way of misfortune.

6.41. *Attaining the worlds of the meritorious and having dwelt there for countless years, he who has fallen from Yoga is born into the dwelling of the radiant and illustrious.*

Krishna reminds Arjuna of his '*illustrious*' birth and status. To continue along his trajectory '*of the radiant and illustrious*' he must act '*uprightly*' (previous verse), but act he must.

6.42. *Or he may be born into a family of wise Yogis, though such a birth is more difficult to attain in the world.*

You get out more than you put in. In acting *'uprightly'* (6.40) Arjuna has a shot at achieving a less martial path, one disengaged from *'this terrible deed of war'* (3.01).

6.43. *There he regains the knowledge from his former body and by virtue of this, strives toward perfection.*

'Strives' shows *'practice of nonattachment'* (6.35) and endeavor (6.36) are always required.

Possessed of knowledge, the family of wise Yogis (previous verse) will impart that knowledge — that level of purity and consciousness attained — lost to the nervous system upon death. The wise Yogis will identify the goal and means to it. He will again *'strive toward perfection.' 'Strive'* implies taking dynamic action, especially now.

6.44. *He is irresistibly carried on, even against his will, by prior practice. Even the aspirant to Yoga rises above those who merely perform rituals.*

The strength of right action is such that even in the absence of knowing its nature to fuel evolution, evolution is pursued and gained. Righteous action engaged is superior to willful passive actions of *'those who* [know the nature of right action but] *merely perform* [go through the motions of] *rituals.'* Act!

6.45. *But the persevering Yogi, purified of sins and perfected through many births, reaches the transcendent goal.*

'The persevering Yogi' acts through thick and thin in the relative by *'practice of nonattachment'* (6.35) and endeavor (6.36). Purification and perfection carry over into rebirth. Act righteously and you will reach the transcendent goal of God Consciousness. Get your mind off philosophy and theory. Act!

6.46. *This Yogi is superior to ascetics, he is superior to the learned, and this Yogi is superior to those performing ritual works. Therefore, be a Yogi.*

Act! Stand up and fight and surpass '*ascetics*' who devote themselves to purification but fail to integrate it into daily life, surpass the '*learned*' who plumb depths of understanding but fail to incorporate them into righteous actions, and even surpass those who curry favor from the gods through '*ritual works*.' Such is the strength of selfless actions in service to drive evolution (Ch 2, 3, 4, and 5).

6.47. *Of all these Yogis, he is most fully united who in faith and devotion honors Me, his inner Self merges into Me.*

'*Of all these Yogis, he is most fully united … who honors*' my teaching of right action through the practice of Karma Yoga (2.45 – 2.47). The solution to resolving doubt, dithering, bondage, and to gaining faith in Me and liberation in God Consciousness? Act! Stand up! Fight! Achieve Cosmic Consciousness and Brahman Consciousness through action alone. Then, let calmness be the means. Merge into God Consciousness.

'*Merges*' speaks to the ongoing process and segues perfectly into Ch 7.

Appendix 3: Know God* — Wisdom from Realization

*As context favors, I use either "God" or "Krishna" for the Supreme Being that creates, protects, and evolves the universe — as the difference between the two is simply a matter of awareness.

Overview of Ch 7:

God's promise: Unprompted by Arjuna, Krishna carries on from Ch 6, deepening the nature of God Consciousness. 1 God promises union with Him by knowing Him completely through His Darshan revealed in the Avatar of these verses. 2 Knowing Him, we achieve his omniscient wisdom. There is nothing left to know about the action wisdom guides. 3 For most seekers, knowing Him is a tough row to hoe. But we have the advantage of seeing God everywhere and having established a working relationship with Him.

God reveals His Hand: Know God through the triad of experience. 4 The experiencer, the process of experiencing and that experienced arise out of His non-transcendent eightfold order of ego, intellect, mind, air, ether, fire, water, and earth.

Experiencer: 1 Ego: lower self unites with higher Self. 2 Intellect: law of increase overrules law of entropy. 3 Mind: awareness of increase unfolds.

Process of Experiencing: 4 Air: out of awareness, dimensions of time and space. 5 Ether: possibilities fill dimensions. 6 Fire: messenger carries forth energy of possibilities.

That Experienced: 7 Water: undifferentiated waves and flow of possibilities. 8 Earth: waves collapse into differentiated form.

Out of God's unknowable transcendent nature emerges: 5 Self => 6 law => 7 impulse => 8 properties => 9 development => 10 seed => 11 dharma => 12 breath. 13 Even understanding

His non-transcendent and transcendent natures, the entire universe, does not recognize His imperishable and eternal nature. There's more to knowing Him.

Maaya: We can't see the forest for the trees. 14 His Divine nature pervades and is veiled by the relative field of life (Maaya). Only by seeking refuge in God can we transcend this delusion of His Divine relative nature. 15 Those fully deluded by Maaya do not seek refuge in God. They seek refuge in pain. They fall into evil actions and demonic tendencies to drag others down to their level of spiritual pain.

Seekers: "Seek and ye shall find." 16 Seekers who honor God with spontaneous gratitude, transcend the delusion of the relative veiling Maaya and find His refuge in the ever-present, thwarting evil actions and demonic tendencies. Seekers fall into two categories: 1) those who seek release from distress, those who seek increased understanding and experience, and those who seek material comfort to pursue spiritual goals and 2) the wise who seek to deepen feelings of gratitude, modesty and fulfillment — and to know Him fully. The first category favors honoring Him with petitionary prayer, while the second favors gratitude. 17 God favors the wise who honor Him alone. So dear to each other, God and the wise form a personal relationship. 18 Through steadfast devotion and engagement of intellect to discern a life of increase, the wise gain His transcendent nature, the Self. 19 At the end of many births, the wise gain clarity of vision which transcends Maaya. Experience of experience falls away.

Personal God: God anticipates our needs to travel His path of evolution and join Him. To achieve this Supreme outcome, belief in Him bestows His Faith and ordains His Desire to achieve. 20 Desiring to gain some finite outcome, we seek support from the higher authority of honored forms (gods) through this or that religious rite. 21 The faith we have in honored forms to influence the nature of our environment comes from Him, the One God. 22 All boons are granted by Him. Acting in His faith, we gain His outcome because the desire to gain it was ordained by Him. 23 However, finite goals fail to fulfill. Honor Him alone and gain infinite fulfillment.

Omniscient in the eternal present: God knows past and future in the eternal present. 24 Deluded by material creation in the finite present, we fail to recognize Krishna as eternal and unsurpassed in wisdom. 25 Further, Yoga-Maaya [seeing union (Yoga) in all relative (Maaya)] conceals Krishna's unborn and imperishable nature. 26 However, limited appreciation of Him — eternal, unsurpassed, unborn, and imperishable — does not restrict His omniscience, which is unbounded by past and future, and the basis of wisdom.

Wisdom: Do as I do. 27 Failing to Honor Him, wisdom based on attractions and aversions guide actions towards greater material wellbeing. Such shallow, lesson-based wisdom falls short of living above sinful wrong actions that retard evolution. 28 Honoring Him, and acting on His Faith and His Desire to achieve His outcome, terminates sinful wrong actions. 29 Lesson-based wisdom falls away. We realize the never-changing source of the ever-changing. We know our Self as His unifying *'transcendent nature, the Self.'* We gain the purity of His Divine omniscient wisdom in our actions. 30 Knowing the principles of the non-transcendent (physical) and transcendent (celestial) realms, we sacrifice our faith, desire and action to Him, the Lord of Sacrifice. We receive His wisdom in His Faith, in His Desire and in His actions and so, unite with Him at the top of the stairs, even in our final act. Wise guides action indeed.

Commentary on Ch 7 verses 1 - 30:

God's promise:

7.01. Without prompting from Arjuna, Krishna continues from His revelation of God Consciousness in Ch 6: *With your mind absorbed in Me, practicing Union, dependent on Me you will know Me completely, hear that without doubt.*

'*Your mind absorbed in Me*' holds the promise of Ch 7. This remarkable pledge to '*know Me completely*' only requires Arjuna to '*hear that* [these verses] *without doubt.*' Krishna lays bare His non-transcendent and transcendent natures, leaving no room for doubt, confusion and uncertainty in a listener prepared for the effect of His revelations.

By '*practicing Union*,' Krishna means listening to Me. Krishna speaks directly into Arjuna's (and our) heightened level of awareness (6.32 - 6.36), strengthening higher Self, verse by verse. Only Krishna can pull off this feat of Divine communication: '*Dependent on Me*' to achieve union with Me and '*know Me completely.*' Such is the blessing of Krishna's Darshan gained through the Avatar of these verses.

7.02. *To you I shall explain this understanding along with providing the experience of it, which once known, nothing further remains to be known in this world of action.*

In beholding Krishna's non-transcendent and transcendent natures through understanding and experience — to include reflection on our past experiences — achieved in these verses, Arjuna comes to know Me fully and gains My wisdom. Then, acting with Divine wisdom, Arjuna will achieve wisdom in Divine action (7.21 - 7.22). And this '*world*' is all about action.

In the previous verse, Krishna stated, '*You will know Me completely.*' In this verse, Krishna lays out His means for fulfilling this promise. Through '*understanding*' wed with '*the experience of it,'* you will gain the knowledge beyond which *'nothing further remains to be known in the world.'* Then, you will act with My wisdom in this world of action. All Krishna requires of Arjuna is *'hear that without doubt'* (previous verse). That is, go with the flow and just listen to my message.

7.03. *Of thousands of men, few strive for perfection. Even among the striving and perfected, scarcely anyone truly knows Me.*

Knowing Him is a tough row to hoe, even for one who is single-minded of purpose, perfected in actions (3.20) and has become the *'Supreme Yogi'* whose consciousness structures knowledge (6.32). Many fall by the wayside. No wonder so few strive for perfection.

But Arjuna is not just *'anyone.'* [And neither are you.] Arjuna and Krishna already have a close relationship to build upon. Krishna sees Arjuna — and you — as His *'devotee and friend'* (4.03). Krishna, the very image of God, is Arjuna's — and our — personal charioteer (revealed in "Personal God," 7.20 – 7.23), here to guide us beyond life's dualities (7.27). Being close to God's image, uniquely positions us to behold Him and truly know Him.

In the following verse, Krishna takes the first step in deepening His relationship with Arjuna (and you) by revealing His nature in the non-transcendent phenomenal world, and in the following eight verses, in the transcendent. Thus, by verse 7.13 we have a handle on Krishna's non-transcendent and transcendent natures.

God reveals His Hand:

7.04. *Earth, water, fire, ether, air, mind, intellect, and ego are My material nature divided eightfold.*

"In the beginning was the Word and the Word was with God and the Word was God." — *John* 1:1

185

The experiencer, the process of experiencing and that experienced come into being *via* His eightfold order. This verse connects the transcendent field of all possibilities with Nature *via* this triad of experience (3.05). Out of Nature leaps all creation by interactions of the three gunas.

The Experiencer:

1) Ego: bounded lower self identifies with unbounded higher Self; the source of all possibilities and creation,

2) Intellect: out of possibilities (previous), discernment favors increase and order (over decrease and entropy),

3) Mind: pure awareness (or pure consciousness) arises, verifying roles of ego and intellect (previous).

Process of experiencing:

4) Air: awareness (previous) opens dimensions of time and space,

5) Ether: primary essence of all possible Veda floods dimensions of time and space (previous),

6) Fire: the messenger carries forth undifferentiated energy of possibilities (previous).

That experienced:

7) Water: undifferentiated energy (previous) precipitates into flowing, undifferentiated waves of the relative.

8) Earth: waves of relative (previous) collapse; first born action, experience and creation; Mother Nature acting through the gunas structures the undifferentiated relative into action, phenomenal experience and phenomenal creation.

7.05. Such is My lower non-transcendent nature; know this to be inferior to My transcendent nature, the Self, which sustains all creation in the universe.

Krishna's non-transcendent nature emerges into being out of His unknowable transcendent. In this and the following seven verses, Krishna reveals His refined, arising and knowable qualities emerging into His eightfold order (previous verse).

The unbounded *'transcendent nature, the Self'* shines through ego, illuminating His *'lower non-transcendent nature,'* sustaining *'all creation in the universe'* *via* the eightfold order ('ego' to 'earth,' previous verse).

7.06. *My transcendent nature births all creatures. Understand this: I am the origin and dissolution of this vast universe.*

The intellect's first order of business sets up His cosmic law of discernment that steers evolution to higher levels: if an action leads to increase and order, thumbs up; if it leads to decrease and dissolution, thumbs down. In His transcendent nature, Krishna discerns increase over entropy, necessary to sustaining never-ending cycles of *'origin and dissolution'* that carry the ball of evolution downfield.

Creatures experience. So, in addition to sustaining *'all creation in the universe'* (previous verse), *'My transcendent nature births all creatures.'* Krishna declares that His transcendent nature births experience, creation and evolution. In this way, He is, by definition, the origin of everything experienced throughout the *'vast universe.'*

Once created, *'intellect'* takes the offensive through the law of order. What He creates, He sustains. What He sustains, He also dissolves into the never-changing aspect of creation whenever that created loses its usefulness to sustain evolution. And out of the never-changing, He again creates. ... This simple three-step law of creating, sustaining and dissolving — all born of His transcendent nature of increase — are part and parcel of the ongoing process of evolution to higher states of spiritual and material wellbeing.

7.07. *Beyond Me nothing exists. On Me all is strung like pearls on a thread.*

Without conscious mind '*nothing exists.*' In the minds eye, Krishna's '*transcendent nature, the Self*' (7.05), emerges a unifying '*thread*' of awareness linking all its creative impulses ('*pearls*'). Conscious mind reveals '*ego*' and '*intellect*' (previous two verses) and completes "the experiencer." '*On Me,*' individual life at its most refined levels of '*ego*' and '*intellect*' begins.

7.08. *I am the fluidity in water, I am the radiance of Sun and Moon, the sacred symbol (Om) in the Vedas, the sound in the air, and manhood of man.*

Dimensions source pure consciousness of mind (previous verse).

'*Fluidity in water*': source relative change.

'*Radiance of Sun and Moon*': source of permanence and impermanence.

'*Om in the Vedas*': source of all possibilities.

'*Sound in the air*': source of name (without form); "In the beginning was the word."

'*Manhood of man*': source of arising power to create and sustain form.

7.09. *I am the pure fragrance in the earth and brightness in fire, the life of all beings and the austerity in ascetics.*

Vital spirit emerging from the power to create and sustain ('*manhood of man,*' previous verse) .

'*Pure fragrance in the earth*': essential spirit of undifferentiated relative.

'*Brightness in fire*': illuminating quality found in all form; the fundamental character sensed by all the senses of perception.

'*Life of all beings*': the defining essence of experiencing.

'*The austerity of ascetics*': the spirit of non-doing (4.13 - 4.14) that underlies all doing and consequently, all creation. *For Me, Arjuna, there is no action in the three worlds I need do. Nor is there anything not attained to attain. Regardless, I engage in action*' through non-doing (3.22) of my Divine nature for increase.

7.10. *Know Me to be the eternal seed of all beings, the intelligence of the intelligent and the radiance of the radiant.*

Expansion; carrying forth increase from the springboard of non-doing ('*austerity of ascetics,*' previous verse).

'*The eternal seed of all beings*': the reseeding property of creation; the fundamental property of endlessly branching one experience into the next.

'*The intelligence of the intelligent*': discriminative rule to expand increase in endlessly evolving experiences.

'*The radiance of the radiant*': quality of expanding energy of increase.

7.11. *And I am strength of the strong, devoid of desire and attachment; in beings I am desire in accord with dharma.*

Promise of relative arising out of '*radiance of the radiant*' (previous verse); quiescent flow before relative; promise of increase latent to change; desire to precipitate change.

'*I am the strength of the strong*': promise of power and firmness underlying all form emerging out of latent change.

'*Devoid of desire and attachment*': wellspring of liberation preceding desire, action and outcome.

'*I am desire in accord with dharma*': the promise increase underlying desire.

7.12. *And finally, know whatever modes of action pertaining to sattva, and also those of rajas and tamas, proceed from me alone. But I am not in them, they are in Me.*

God's Love underlies promise (previous verse) and informs Mother Nature to breathe name into the three gunas and create form.

Through the triad of experience, we create action and experience *via* the three gunas of Nature (7.04). True enough, increase (sattva) and also spur to action (rajas) and check and retard (tamas) have their origin in Krishna, the Self (7.05). But being the eternal non-doer outside the field of desire and action (previous verse) '*I am not in them.* Instead,' '*they are in Me,*' the pure source of increase that flows from My transcendent nature, the Self. That is, Krishna in his Divine transcendent nature of increase born of love can exist without the gunas of Nature, but the gunas of Nature cannot exist without Krishna's love, '*they are in Me*' and consequently, all creation flows out of love from transcendent Me.

7.13. *The entire universe, deluded by the influence born of the three Gunas, does not recognize My imperishable nature which is higher than them and eternal.*

We '*recognize*' by senses and mind, which are themselves of '*the entire universe*' born of the three gunas (previous verse). Senses and mind experience and understand the phenomenal world, and sustain evolution and wellbeing. '*Deluded by the influence born of the three Gunas,*' senses and mind look outward into the ever-changing and transient field of action. To guide our actions towards wellbeing, they focus on material creation of His lower non-transcendent nature (7.04), rather than look inward to see '*My imperishable nature which is higher than them and eternal*' (7.05 - 7.12).

In addition, we do not '*recognize*' His '*imperishable nature*' in the field of action '*born of the three Gunas*' because He is '*not in them* [not in the gunas and the field of actions they engender],' *rather they* [the Gunas] *are in Me*' (previous verse).

The Gunas, being in Me, all relative created by them is Divine (following verse).

Maaya:

7.14. *Divine is this Maaya of Mine, comprised of the Gunas and veiled by them. Only those who seek My refuge, transcend this delusion.*

'*Maaya*' is God's inherent expression of the entire relative field of existence as perceived by the senses, mind and intellect. This '*Maaya*' is '*comprised of the Gunas,*' who '*are in Me*' (7.12). Being '*in Me*' and the source of all My creation, the Gunas express My Divine nature in their relative field of existence. Hence, '*Divine is this Maaya of Mine.*'

This preeminent Divine nature of the Gunas pervades the Guna's influence on the relative field, that is, on '*Maaya.*' The never-changing Divine and ever-changing '*Maaya*' go hand-in-glove. But this ever-changing '*Maaya*' veils its more refined never-changing Divine nature.

Acting on the level of *Maaya*'s relative and transient nature, we can never '*transcend this delusion*' of the relative because acting engages the gunas and sustain their veil over Divine Maaya. '*Only those who seek My refuge, transcend this delusion*' (7.16). Delusion transcended, we see His '*transcendent nature, the Self*' (7.05) within the non-transcendent '*material nature divided eightfold*' (7.04). That is, we see God everywhere and at all times in this Divine '*Maaya*' of this phenomenal world.

7.15. *Evil doers, the lowest of men, deluded by Maaya do not seek Me, dependent as they are on demonic tendencies.*

Fail to transcend delusion (previous verse), live delusion. Rather than seek '*My imperishable nature*' as the means to transcend this delusion, *'evil doers'* look to *'Maaya'* as real and opportunity. They seek the delusion of *'Maaya'* as a refuge from their natural desire to seek increase in spiritual wellbeing and to travel the path to know God (7.03).

Agents of entropy, *'evil doers'* retard evolution in spiritual and material wellbeing (2.47). Lacking human qualities of community, empathy, brotherly love, and a sense of wonder, they selfishly choose to seek nothing beyond *'Maaya.'* Dependent on their habit of exercising *'demonic tendencies'* to retard evolution, *'evil doers'* seek the undoing of others, taking pleasure in bringing others down to their level, *'the lowest of men.'*

Rather than honor God (following verse), *'evil doers,'* who depend *'on demonic tendencies'* to find transient pleasure over pain, choose to dishonor Him: *'deluded by Maaya* [they] *do not seek Me'* as worthy of knowing and as the ultimate refuge beyond the spiritual pain of delusion they feel.

Seekers:

"Seek and ye shall find." — *Mathew 7:7.*

7.16. *Four kinds of benevolent men honor Me: the distressed, seekers of knowledge, seekers of wealth, and the man of wisdom.*

To *'honor Me'* in its highest form is to show sincere thankfulness for guidance and revealing *'My transcendent nature, the Self'* (7.05). Spontaneous gratitude to God transcends the space-time delusion of *'Maaya'* (7.14), finds *'My refuge'* in the ever-present, and thwarts negative feelings and wrong actions (*'Evil doers'* and *'demonic tendencies,'* previous verse).

In contrast to the negative character of *'evil doers,'* *'benevolent men'* intend to do good and perform right actions to support spiritual and material evolution (2.47). They *'honor Me'* by recognizing Me to the degrees of gratitude they feel.

For four different reasons, they *'seek My refuge'* (7.14).

The first three lack fulfillment and seek release, increased understanding and experience, and comfort to pursue spiritual pursuits, respectively. *'The distressed,'* backed into a corner, see Me as a way out and seek refuge from material poverty and turbulence in life. *'Seekers of knowledge'* acknowledge My transcendent and non-transcendent natures; they seek refuge to gain understanding and experience, and smooth the path forward based on deepening knowledge of Me. *'Seekers of wealth'* desire to improve spiritual wellbeing on the foundation of prosperity; they seek to *'transcend delusion'* (7.14) aided by material comfort and so, focus their time, attention and resources on Me alone.

These first three *'kinds of benevolent men'* tend to favor petitionary prayer and in this way, honor God as the supreme benefactor in the phenomenal world. Their notion of fulfillment tends to favor the material over the spiritual.

Rather than petition God, *'the man of wisdom'* alone gains fulfillment in honoring Him by seeking to deepen feelings of gratitude, modesty and fulfillment. *'The man of wisdom'* truly seeks to know God, even though he is uncertain of what knowing God ultimately means. In seeking fulfillment, he favors the spiritual over the material. Though he can be a bit fuzzy on what "spiritual" means, he seeks God as the means to his fulfillment. His prays more to express thankfulness than to petition increase in the phenomenal world.

7.17. *Among these benevolent men, the man of wisdom, eternally steadfast, and devoted to the One is preeminent. I am dear to him and he is dear to Me.*

Krishna admonishes Arjuna not to dilute devotion across a plurality of gods. Why spread honor across gods, who themselves behold the One God as Supreme? *Devoted to the One* [God]' achieve preeminence among seekers and achieve union with Me. [More on this theme of One God in verses 7.20 – 7.23.]

The 'man of wisdom' is enlightened in God Consciousness and sees Him everywhere (6.32). 'Devoted to the One,' who is everything and constitutes everything, the wise steadfastly focus on taking refuge in 'the One'. They lavishly honor 'the One' and 'the One' alone. The devoted 'man of wisdom' faithfully walks the path of indeterminant length (7.03). Seeking refuge in Me above all else (previous verse), the wise develop a personal relationship with God, 'I am dear to him,' and because My Divine wisdom of increase in evolution guides him towards the supreme goal of knowing Me, 'he is dear to Me.'

7.18. *All these benevolent men are exalted. But the man of wisdom is My own Self. His steadfast intellect engages to become established in Me, the supreme goal.*

'All these [four] are exalted' above non-seekers and 'evil doers.' They see the value of higher states of spiritual and material wellbeing, and actively seek to achieve them by honoring Me in their own way (7.16). However, because of their lower levels of consciousness, the first three petition Him to provide:

- a way out of dark corners of spiritual and material poverty,
- intermediate levels of understanding and experience to smooth the journey,
- comforting wealth to focus resources on Him.

That is, 'the distressed, seekers of knowledge and seekers of wealth' see the steps in front of them but not God at the top of the stairs.

On the other hand, the 'man of wisdom is My own Self.' Guided by My Divine wisdom to achieve union with Me (previous verse), the man of wisdom's 'steadfast intellect' ceaselessly engages in discerning increase in evolution to know Me. Through 'steadfast' engagement of his 'intellect' devoted to knowing Me, the man of wisdom gains a personal relationship with Me. 'Eternally steadfast, and devoted to the

One [God]' (previous verse), 'the man of wisdom' unites with Me and 'is My own Self.' That is, he 'gains my transcendent nature, the Self' (7.05) by steadfastly engaging his intellect to climb the steps of increase in front of him and unite with Me in My Divine wisdom at the top of the stairs.

7.19. *At the end of many births, the man of wisdom takes refuge in Me, knowing Vasudeva (Krishna) is all. Such a great soul is rare indeed.*

This verse validates efforts to strive for perfection (7.03)

Only 'a*t the end of many births, the man of wisdom takes refuge in Me.*' Clarity of vision overtakes '*Maaya*' and transcends delusion through '*steadfast intellect*' (previous verse). '*Vasudeva*' conveys the essential Oneness that is everything and constitutes everything. The man of wisdom not only transcends '*Maaya,*' he gains Oneness with it. Consequently, there is no difference among the pearls on the thread (7.07). The medium of experience and gradations among actions evaporate. '*Knowing Vasudeva*' transcends experience; experience of experience fades.

'*Such a great soul is rare indeed*' supplants '*Of thousands of men, few strive for perfection.*' (7.03). '*Great soul*' supersedes '*men.*' Men experience. Soul is. Higher Self supersedes lower self. Through Krishna's '*transcendent nature, the Self*' (7.05) the '*great soul*' breaks free from experience (7.04).

Personal God:

7.20. *Men whose wisdom has been carried away by this or that desire resort to other gods, following this or that religious rite, compelled by their own nature.*

'*Men whose wisdom has been carried away by this or that desire*' to gain a finite goal — say, buying a house, gaining a fruitful relationship, or winning an election — lose steadfast intellect, devotion to the One God, preeminence, knowing

Vasudeva, and the rarity of a great soul (previous three verses). Having limited belief in God and failing to understand their personal relationship with Him, they engage in '*this or that religious rite*' and '*resort to other gods*,' '*compelled by their own nature*' to gain support from some higher authority to achieve a finite goal.

7.21. *Whosoever desires to act with belief in whatever honored form, on him I bestow steady faith.*

'*Honored form*' refers to various '*other gods*' (previous verse). The gods represent favorable forces of Nature, for example ('*honored form*' in parentheses), fortune (*Lakshmi*), success (*Saraswati*), remover of obstacles (*Ganesha*). By honoring a specific god in '*whatever honored form*,' we gain measures of its influence in our lives. [Today, perhaps '*honored form*[s]' include '*belief*' in various *isms*: environmentalism, educationalism, scientism, atheism, politicisms, and other stratagems to execute selfish actions and achieve '*enjoyment and power*' over others (2.43). Stratagems also require '*following this or that religious rite*' with firm belief, devotion and evangelizing.]

'*Honored form*[s]' are impersonal. Through supplication and offering ('*this or that religious rite*,' previous verse), we ask them to influence our environment to support achieving desired material outcome. But they do not support evolution to higher wellbeing and the Supreme goal beyond the material to infinitude in union with God. To that, they are a distraction. In fact, we don't expect them to bring us to God. Focused on finite outcomes, these '[impersonal] *honored form*[s]' remain aloof to our evolution, wellbeing and infinite nature — and as we shall see in verse 7.23, hold our nose to the grindstone of impression-desire-action (2.39). A personal relationship with us is not on '*honored form*['s] job description. Fact is, '*honored form*[s]' are not here for you. God is. The One God loves you.

Not all seekers have the vision to honor the One God. But, nevertheless, even for those who lack vision, and resort to '*whatever honored form*[s],' God Himself bestows '*steady faith*' that the desire will be fulfilled.

7.22 He, who, engaged with My endowed faith, who desires to gain from that form receives his desires because those desires are ordained by Me.

Faith seeds desires and outcomes in accord with evolution.

'*Faith*' resides in God's domain (previous verse). God not only endows '*faith*' to achieve some finite outcome through '*whatever honored form*' (previous verse), but also ordains '*desire.*' And '*because those desires are ordained by Me,*' God bestows the desired outcome. Through belief in God, we open channels of Faith through which His desires and His outcomes flow. Simultaneously, we feel as though faith and desires are our own doing, while at the same time, we witness actions guide us toward the outcome.

Getting desires fulfilled by God through '*whatever honored form*' sounds tempting. Why bother with the arduous trek (7.03) to unite with the One God? Why bother to reach beyond finite goals and '*other gods*?'

Because there's a catch, a big one.

7.23. But fleeting is the fruit gained for those with limited understanding. To the gods the god worshiping go. Those who honor Me will surely come to Me.

"Thus saith the Lord, the King of Israel and his redeemer, the Lord of hosts: I am the first, and I am the last; besides me there is no God." — *Isaiah* 44:6

There is more to life than '*fleeting*' finite goals. While necessary to the nuts and bolts of survival and living a life of increase in wellbeing, finite goals never fulfill. In fact, having attention on finite goals, by themselves, leads to bondage to action and living on the horizontal plane of life (see cycles of impression-desire-action, 2.39).

Those with 'limited understanding' of the True source of faith, desire and outcome (previous two verses) 'resort to other gods' (7.20). And 'To the gods the god worshiping go' again and again and again ad infinitum, seeking finite goals, stuck on the horizontal plane of life, bound to unfulfilling experiences and unrealized expectations, living in ignorance, eternally seeking fulfillment, even though 'honored form[s]' never advertise powers to fulfill.

Verses 7.20 - 7.22 lift the veil of 'limited understanding.' Within the finite lies the infinite. Within gaining a finite goal lies the unbounded One God. Faith, desire, and outcome are His doing, not the gods, not ours. Knowing through understanding and experience that His infinite nature (His 'transcendent nature, the Self,' 7.05) lies in gaining the finite ('My material nature divided eightfold,' 7.04), we naturally come to honor Him with gratitude.

All gratitude lives in the present. Gratitude to God is superlative and transcends the delusion of all finite and relative (7.14). Attention in the eternal present, we break bondage to action, rise on the vertical plane of life and naturally 'come to' Him. That's all it takes to sprout wings of faith: gratitude to God.

Up close and personal. Honor God through gratitude and automatically, His Faith, Desire and Outcome become our faith, desire and outcome. And as we shall see in the following verses, his omniscient wisdom becomes our wisdom. Only a loving and personal God could bond such an intimate relationship to anticipate and meet our needs to achieve higher material and spiritual wellbeing. To travel His path, to come to Him and know Him completely, and to unite with Him, God only asks for belief in Him (7.21) and to get the job done, recognition of Him through gratitude for all He does to meet our natural and gnawing need to achieve fulfillment.

These verses clearly illustrate the Gita's monotheism and religious tolerance.

Omniscient in the eternal present:

7.24. Not knowing my transcendent nature, the unwise see Me as manifest, unaware of My higher unmanifest nature which is imperishable and unsurpassed.

Lord Krishna's Divine nature is transcendent, eternal and unsurpassed in its wisdom. However, those who have yet to finalize wisdom (7.30) perceive only through the restrictions of the five senses and bounded mind (previous verse). Consequently, they perceive the unmanifest and eternal as manifest, transitory and ordinary; they fail to see My transcendent nature in My non-transcendent eightfold order (7.04 - 7.05). Deluded by the Maaya of material creation in the finite present (7.14 - 7.15), God's Divine nature — *'Divine is this Maaya of mine'* (7.24) — appears manifest, whereas in its transcendent Reality it is *'unmanifest,' 'imperishable,'* and *'unsurpassed'* in its wisdom. His wisdom — His guidance in our action — lives forever.

7.25. Being entirely concealed by Yoga-Maaya, I am not apparent to all. This deluded world does not recognize Me as unborn and unchanging.

Even in God Consciousness Maaya's delusion persists. *'Yoga-Maaya'*: we see God everywhere (6.32), but yet, the "everywhere" we see is itself manifest and perishable. We fail to see the unmanifest and imperishable in Divine Maaya itself, *'Divine is this Maaya of mine'* (7.24). Something is still missing in our perception of God, even in God Consciousness. In part, the novelty of seeing union (Yoga) everywhere in the relative field of life (*'Maaya,'* 7.12) helps to conceal His *'unborn and unchanging nature.'* So to speak, we have to get over it.

Krishna remains unmanifest in the manifest perception of Him. An Avatar of Vishnu seen in human form, His unmanifest nature is *'not apparent to all.'* Where mental limitations force perceiving in the space and time of the finite ever-changing present, 'This deluded world [of limited perception in the finite present] does not recognize Me as unborn and unchanging,' as is all phenomenal existence.

7.26. I know the departed and the living beings and those yet to be. But no one knows Me fully.

Why bother with honoring forces of nature and gaining some measure of the 'honored form's' restricted sphere of influence (7.20 - 7.23)? Instead, know God. Fuel your wisdom with His omniscience expressed in His faith, His desire and His outcome. Honor Him and the layers of Maaya peel away. All is revealed.

Limiting our perception of Him does not restrict His omniscient perception, which is unbounded by past and future. To illustrate His unmanifest transcendent nature (7.05; previous verse), Krishna reveals His Self as unbounded by Maaya of material creation in the finite present. 'I know the departed and the living beings and those yet to be.' That is, I am omniscient of past and future in the eternal present.

'But no one,' who remains individualized as 'one' of lower self, who spins their wheels by worshiping other 'honored form[s],' and who has yet to unite with Me, 'knows Me fully.' We cannot know God from a distance or by reason and abstraction. Surely, we cannot know God when veiled by His 'divine Maaya' of material creation in the finite present. Those susceptible to 'Yoga-Maaya' (previous verse) will necessarily distort His unmanifest and transcendent nature to the transient finite present, a distortion which short-circuits union, knowing Him fully and gaining His omniscient wisdom.

Wisdom:

7.27. Due to dualities arising from attraction and aversion, all beings fall into confusion at birth.

Without God's omniscience (previous verse), we fall into sinful wrong actions that retard evolution in spiritual and material wellbeing (see right and wrong actions, 2.47).

From birth, our senses, minds and intellects guide actions toward greater wellbeing based on attractive and aversive experiences. As a rule, we favor the attractive (say, owning gold) which renders happiness and avoid the aversive (say, snake bite) which renders unhappiness. Hopefully, attractive experiences outweigh aversive ones, and in our measured way, we evolve along our path to greater happiness and wellbeing.

Through intellectually understanding philosophy of action and applying it to life's lessons, we modify our behavior based on our attractive and aversive experiences. Gradually, we become wiser with age. But self-induced behavioral modification lacks prescience to hold actions on a true course of evolution through new and challenging experiences. Despite our best efforts, we waste precious time floundering.

The full sweep of having God's omniscience guide actions lies beyond our ken and ability to self-apply naturally. Out of innocence, we 'fall into confusion at birth' and to varying degrees, remain confused due to the incompleteness and fragility of lesson-based wisdom. In addition, reasoning our course of action through attraction and aversion fails to account for long-term consequences. Achieving greater wellbeing is often a crapshoot. At best, we stumble along and screw things up from time-to-time; at worst, we fall into league with 'evil doers' (7.15), lose balance of mind (2.48) and trip off the smooth path of evolution.

7.28. *Those whose sinful acts end, whose actions are pure, liberated from the confusing power of opposites, honor Me with resolve.*

Our personal God knows what's best for our evolution. God's omniscient wisdom, achieved by acting in our belief and in His

Faith and Desire (7.20 – 7.22), 'ends' lesson-based wisdom and liberates us 'from the confusing power of opposites.' Following His guiding hand, naturally making right choices and performing actions that support evolution in the long-term, slams the brakes on 'sinful acts.' Our actions seem to go of their own accord. Steady faith dawns. In the groove, we spontaneously feel grateful.

Instinctively honoring God with gratitude — 'honor Me with resolve' — plants our feet firmly in the eternal present. Gratitude balances us on the path and liberates us from shallow wisdom based on 'dualities arising from attraction and aversion' (previous verse). Consequently, resolute gratitude purifies actions to achieve God's cosmic plan to 'come to Me' (7.23) and once at His side, to know 'Me fully' (7.26). Over time, gratitude deepens, strengthens, permeates all action, and establishes itself; the present achieved in spontaneous gratitude becomes eternal.

7.29. *Those who strive for relief from old age and death, having taken refuge in Me, know Brahman thoroughly, as well as the Self (Adhyaatma) and all action (karma).*

'*Those who strive for relief from old age and death*' refers to those who seek to know '*My transcendent nature, the Self*' (7.05) in My non-transcendent eightfold order (7.04). They '*strive for perfection*' in action to evolve (7.03) and ultimately, seek liberation from rebirth.

'*Having taken refuge in Me*' by honoring Me with gratitude, we live in the eternal present (previous verse). We achieve His omniscient wisdom in action through His Faith and His Desire (7.20 – 7.23). Futile lesson-based wisdom guided by attraction and aversion loses purpose and falls by the wayside.

We see everything (His non-transcendent nature, 7.04) and that which constitutes everything (his '*transcendent nature,*' 7.05). Being on the ground floor, as it were, we see nonaction in action and action in nonaction: by experiencing God everywhere, through all the senses, we '*know Brahman*

[Oneness, (4.18)] *thoroughly'*. We know our supreme *'Self (Adhyaatma)'* as Krishna's *'transcendent nature, the Self'* (7.05). Through intellectual understanding and recognizing His guidance in past and present experiences, we know His Divine nature pervades *'all action (karma)'* (7.04).

7.30. *Those who know Me as governing principle of the physical realm (Adhibhuta) and simultaneously as governing principle of the celestial realm (Adhidaiva), as well as the Lord of Sacrifice, their minds know Me even in the hour of death.*

At long last, this final verse steps up from *'liberated from the bondage of rebirth'* and *'go to the end of rebirth'* (2.51, 5.17). But, we step up to where? *'Liberated'* to what? What lies beyond the *'end of rebirth?'*

We know our supreme Self (*Adhyaatma*), which underlies His non-transcendent and transcendent natures (7.05, 7.18, 7.19, previous verse). Consequently, we *'simultaneously'* know God's governing principle of increase in evolution (7.04, 7.06, 7.12, and *'the man of wisdom,'* 7.17 – 7.18) in His non-transcendent *'physical realm (Adhibhuta)'* and the governing principle of love (7.12) in His transcendent *'celestial realm (Adhidaiva).'* In belief we take refuge in these principles and surrender faith, desire and outcome to the *'Lord of Sacrifice'* (7.20 – 7.23), gaining God's omniscient wisdom to guide our actions to the highest levels of wellbeing (7.24 – 7.26).

Knowing God's governing principle in the *'physical realm'* guides our final act. Eyes lifted in expectation of increase we see God at the top of the stairs. We step up to God's *'celestial realm'* and in love, know Him completely. The promise of this chapter kept. Wisdom guides action indeed!

"Where are the songs of spring? Ay, Where are they?
Think not of them, thou hast thy music too,"
John Keats, *To Autumn.*

Appendix 4: States of Consciousness in a Nutshell

Principle criteria for seven states of consciousness. Some experiences of higher states of consciousness overlap.

Sleep Consciousness: Unaware.

Dream Consciousness: Subjective awareness of memory during sleep.

Waking Consciousness: Action overshadows awareness of transcendent higher Self.

Transcendental Consciousness: Experience of liberation when selflessly serving others' desires.

Cosmic Consciousness: Aware of contented higher Self during sleeping, dreaming and diverse activities of waking state consciousness.

Brahman Consciousness: We see Oneness of Brahman in everything. Calmness separates higher Self from activity.

God Consciousness: Achieved through calmness, happiness abiding in the heart dissolves separation between higher Self and activity. We see God everywhere.

Union with God: Faith.

About the Author

Once upon a time I lived in northern Maine and picked potatoes. My brother and sister picked potatoes. All able bodies living north of the Nine-Mile Woods — other school-age kids, the indigent, the unemployable, housewives assisted by toddlers — picked potatoes too.

We'd arrive in early-morning darkness at the frost-covered field to the sound of the tractor firing up. Farmers paid us 20 cents a barrel. On a good day, I picked 25 barrels. Most pickers were more ambitious. With earnings, we bought winter clothing to tilt into blowing snow at freezing temperatures.

One day, I stood from stoop labor and looked across the field to the small pond bordering it. On the far side, a Great Blue Heron fed among tall reeds.

The veil lifted. Space-time collapsed. Unifying effulgence backlit everything: the sky, the pond, the unpicked potatoes, the sound of the tractor, the scent of loamy earth. I saw Oneness in all. I felt familiar with all. I knew all.

We can argue about my experience of knowing all. But I knew one thing for certain. I didn't see a future in picking potatoes.

In time, I joined the Army. With the draft breathing down my neck, it was a natural enough move. My life began.

Unknowingly, it was a step in the direction of spiritual evolution. My eyes opened to the value of service in a wider world. I had three experiences that revealed my life's koan and started a 50-year quest to solve it.

First, following orders liberated me from selfish individuality. Well, at least for some of the time, anyway. Serving others innocently detached me from petty concerns about transgression, beer money, The Girls, training cycles, fears, and my uncertain future.

Of course, I fought these feelings of liberation. *'This is not the way it's supposed to be!'* But undeniably, there it was, a sense of inner peace and familiarity amidst the dull-set patterns of disciplined, olive-drab life and moils of rough-and-tumble Special Forces training. There were shades of the Great Blue Herron.

Second, in Vietnam, I served on an A-Team in The Valley of Death. The soul of an A-Team is trust. Trust engenders sacrifice and sacrifice is service on steroids. Elevated above the fray, I detached from strong emotions. Instinctive, selfless actions shoved fear to the back burner. Service on steroids, indeed.

War lopped off the head of self-importance. Humbled. Reincarnated. Emancipated.

Third: Getting out I felt stronger in all ways. I believed in myself. An invisible hand helped me navigate life. I flowed along more than stumbled. True enough, life wasn't a bed of roses. I carried baggage. But somehow, my past made perfect sense and I looked forward. I took my own path. The Great Blue strode ahead on long legs.

In time, scattered thoughts about moving with the flow clarified into a koan. *'How had I been uplifted and strengthened through acts of service?'* I know, my koan was not as flashy as "What is the sound of one hand clapping?"

But my koan was personal. It had momentum and held my attention in quiet, inner ways. The koan was always there, lurking in my subconscious. It popped into thought at odd times: on redeyes from Frankfurt to Sao Paulo, slapping mosquitoes in Cameroon, reading a two-course menu in a Michelin starred restaurant, watching my bush plane's shadow drift across frozen and dusty corners of the world.

My 'aha' moment. Seeing the forest for the trees. Literally.

Fifty years on, the answer popped into my head out of the dome of California's Tiepolo sky. Drying the breakfast dishes, I idly surveyed the intersection where the golden oak savannah of my meadow merged into the dark greens of Douglas firs and redwoods, puzzling about a verse on bondage to action in the *Bhagavad Gita*, a constant companion since my days in Vietnam.

The scales fell from my eyes. Clarity backlit everything. I beamed back.

But being the analytical type, it didn't take long to wonder, '*Was I correct*?'

The intuitive '*Yes*' came instantly. Like slipping into the warm protected waters of my private lagoon, it just felt right.

The evidentiary '*Yes*' lay in deeper waters. I knew what felt right was not necessarily so. Pearls of wisdom had morphed into plastic baubles upon deeper examination before.

Thing is, I just couldn't avoid the nagging question, '*Does my answer meet scriptural authority*?' Naturally, I thought about the *Bhagavad Gita* and then, the daunting task of plumbing its deeper depths. '*Hey, why go there*?'

Regardless, I pinched off my nostrils and jumped in. Damn the deeper waters. I took the *Gita* one word at a time. I sifted through multiple word meanings, learned to appreciate context and easily dismissed the drone of repetitive, less than insightful copycat commentaries.

Fitting my understanding and experience into the symbolism and narrative of Krishna's teachings took time, mountain ranges of patience, introspection, solitude, and most importantly, wings of faith.

The Great Blue Herron lifted me to new heights. My horizons expanded. Below, fields of potatoes bordered by ponds and streams and forest unending. To the west, the bulge of Appalachians, farther west snowcapped peaks of Rockies and

High Sierras. Ahead, the boundless Pacific and other shore. Climbing through cruise altitude, I share the Supreme Secret of this ancient Yoga of action with you.

In affirmation, magic.

Keith R Parker, Angel Fire, New Mexico

Printed in Great Britain
by Amazon

21171763R00119